# Paradox, Dialectic, and System

# PARADOX, DIALECTIC, and SYSTEM

A Contemporary Reconstruction of
the Hegelian Problematic

HOWARD P. KAINZ

THE PENNSYLVANIA STATE UNIVERSITY PRESS
University Park and London

*142*
*K13p*

The verses on page 41 are from ''Little Gidding'' in *Four Quartets* by
T. S. Eliot, copyright 1943 by T. S. Eliot; renewed 1971 by Esme
Valerie Eliot. Reprinted by permission of Harcourt Brace Jovanovich,
Inc., and by Faber and Faber Ltd., London.

Library of Congress Cataloging-in-Publication Data

Kainz, Howard P.
Paradox, dialectic, and system.

Bibliography: p.
Includes index.
1. Paradox. 2. Dialectic. 3. Hegel, Georg Wilhelm
Friedrich, 1770–1831.     I. Title.
BC199.P2K35     1988     142     86–43036
ISBN 0-271-00499-1

# Contents

Preface     vii

1    Some "External Considerations"     1
*Logic, Semantics, Grammar, and*
   *Paradox*     1
*Mathematics, Science, and Paradox*     10
*Logico-Philosophical Considerations*     14

2    Self-Consciousness and the
   Origins of Dialectic     22
*Ordinary Logic and the*
   *Subject/Object Distinction*     22
*Reflection and Dialectic*     26
*Dialectic and Ordinary Logic*     30
*Systematization of Dialectical Logic?*     33

3    Paradox and the Congruent
   Philosophical Expression of
   Dialectic     35
*Dialectical Logic and Paradox*     35
*The Varieties of Paradox*     37
*Philosophical Paradox*     42
*Philosophical Paradox and*
   *Dialectical Logic*     44

4    The Systematization of Dialectic          49
     *An Initial Dilemma for the*
          *Systematizer*                       50
     *Modern Attempts at Synthesis*            52
     *Systematization in Philosophy*           54
     *Dialectical Philosophy and*
          *Systematization*                    56
5    Hegel's Dialectical-Paradoxical
     System                                    75
     *The Various Senses of "System" in*
          *Hegel*                              78
     *The Originary Paradox in Hegel's*
          *System*                             83
     *Corollary, Derivative, and Subsidiary*
          *Paradoxes*                          89
     *Hegel's System as Paradox: The*
          *Circle of Circles*                  93
     *Hegel's* Phenomenology of Spirit *and*
          *Circularity*                        98
     *Circularity and Philosophical*
          *Paradox*                            108
Conclusion                                     111
Notes                                          114
Bibliography                                   127
Index                                          131

# Preface

This book is the result of my encounter in Hegel-interpretation
with some originally scattered problems, which gradually organized themselves as a confluence of problems that had best be
considered in interconnection with each other: Was Hegel right
about the necessity for a system in philosophy, and the "necessity" of the various parts of the system which he eventually
constructed? Are there any essential differences between a
"dialectical" system and an ordinary nondialectical but logically concatenated system? What is the significance of the
literally hundreds of paradoxical assertions to be found in
Hegel's *Phenomenology of Spirit* and *Encyclopedia of the
Philosophical Sciences?* Could these paradoxes be associated
with the use of a dialectical methodology, in perhaps the same
way that the monadic assertorial proposition is connected with
the procedures of ordinary formal logic? And if so, do the
paradoxes which are thus generated possess any organized
interconnections among themselves? Are the systematic connections to be found in a dialectical system susceptible to any
kind of *sui generis* formalization in the way that ordinary
thought patterns are subject to the categorizations and analyses
of formal logic? And finally, might it not be the case that
dialectic, paradox, and system are necessarily interrelated, so
that, for example, a dialectic without paradox would be suspect,
and philosophically significant dialectical paradoxes might be
optimally presented in a system which recaptured any natural or

logical organization (subordination and coordination) existing among themselves?

But concentration on dialectic, the systematization of dialectic, and/or paradoxical formulations is by no means an exclusive feature of Hegel's philosophy. It is to be found as a somewhat cyclical phenomenon in and out of philosophy from ancient times to the present. This realization led me outside the Hegelian system to an investigation of the problematic in its larger dimensions, in order to lay the theoretical foundations for a closer systematic investigation of the similar problematic embodied specifically in Hegel's philosophy. Thus, I begin my analysis, somewhat analogously to the way that Hegel begins in the Preface to his *Phenomenology*, with an analysis of some current and historical developments in empirical science, mathematics, logic, and philosophy. This is followed, in chapters 2 and 3, by a theoretical reformulation of the above-mentioned problematic, in a fashion largely independent of any Hegelian moorings. And then, in chapters 4 and 5, Hegel's system is presented as a result, but not necessarily the last or the best result, of an evolution of the problematic in question.

The research for this book over the last six years has been assisted by a series of grants and awards: A sabbatical in the fall of 1979; a Marquette University Summer Fellowship in the summer of 1980; a Fulbright award to work at the Hegel-Archiv in Bochum, West Germany, during the academic year 1981–82; some released time awarded by the Executive Committee of my department in 1984; and a second Summer Fellowship in 1985. I am very grateful that all these disparate powers thought it worthwhile to fund an investigation which seemed to lead me insidiously out of those parameters of Hegel scholarship I had been more accustomed to. But, as will be seen from chapter 5 and the Conclusion, I have "come back" with a renewed, if more nuanced, appreciation of the Hegelian undertaking.

I would like to thank Heidi Malmquist, and Wolfgang Bonsiepen and Walter Jaeschke, who helped me in the preparation of the initial German version of chapters 1–3, which was originally published as a monograph in 1984 in *Hegel-Studien;* Tom

Rockmore, who read and critiqued an intermediate stage of the book; Joseph O'Malley, Michael Wreen, Michael McCanles, Stanley Bashkin, and Thaddeus Burch, who read and commented on certain parts of the book; Kathy Hawkins of Marquette Word Processing Services for preparation of the final English manuscript; and graduate assistants Bob Abele, Bradley Wronski, Janette Hodge, Douglas Lampshire, and Maureen Milligan, who proofread the various stages of the manuscript. The inevitable imperfections remaining cannot be ascribed to the assistance I have received.

# 1

## Some "External Considerations"

> The inner necessity that knowing should be [philosophical] science lies in its nature, and only the systematic exposition of philosophy itself provides it. But the *external* necessity, so far as it is grasped in a general way, setting aside accidental matters of person and motivation, is the same as the inner.
> —Hegel, *The Phenomenology of Spirit*, Preface

Although the internal interrelationships and organization of philosophical considerations are of the utmost importance, one should not expect a complete dissymmetry between philosophy and its logico-mathematical and scientific milieux; and, in fact, philosophical approaches or positions may receive added corroboration, if not essential demonstrative premises, from areas usually compartmentalized as external to the ambit of philosophy proper. With this in mind, we begin with an examination of certain developments in logic, mathematics, and the physical sciences which may have a bearing on our investigation of paradox and dialectic.

## *Logic, Semantics, Grammar, and Paradox*

Paradoxes have generally been considered an embarrassment in the history of philosophy. Some classical scholars spent the best part of a lifetime trying to make sense of "this statement is false" (or other variations of Eubulides' famous "liar paradox," such as "all knowledge is doubtful" and "all rules have exceptions"); and it is thought that at least one or two may have come to a premature demise as a result of their frustrations in this endeavor.

Although such paradoxes have frequently been refuted on the logical-syntactical and/or semantic levels, it would seem that there are some antecedent grammatical problems in even *formulating* the paradoxes in such a way as to be susceptible to logical analysis. For example, it is hard to find a satisfactory formulation of the liar paradox. In the formulation, "this statement is false," the "this" of ordinary language does *not* conventionally refer to the statement in which it appears but to some antecedent statement; so that one who hears this formulation may reasonably ask, "*which* statement?" In the classical formulation, "Epimenides the Cretan prophet says that all Cretans are liars," it may be taken for granted that Epimenides is referring to all ordinary Cretans and *not* to himself, as when a religious reformer states, "our church is corrupt," referring, of course, to other members of the church. If Epimenides came right out and said, "I am a liar," we might safely presume that he was referring to all his other statements, but *not* to this one— as a chronic liar who comes to his senses and makes his first true statement about his past delinquencies (to be a liar does not necessarily mean that one lies all the time). Even if Epimenides states, "the statement I am making right now is a lie," we may utilize Gilbert Ryle's "namely-rider" to ask: "namely, which statement?" If he, on a sudden inspiration, draws a rectangle on the present page and writes within it, "The statement in the rectangle on page 2 of this book is false"—we might still ask, "which statement?" "We only see one statement on this page." "Where is the false statement it's referring to?" Even if, in a final attempt at graphic demonstration, he writes, "*This* sentence is false," circles the sentence, and draws an arrow ascending from "*This*" and then circling back down to point to the circle containing the whole sentence—this would be merely equivalent grammatically to saying, "*This* sentence, namely, '*This* sentence is false,' is false." The sentence in the single quotes, again, could not refer to itself but, at most, to another implied sentence, illustrated by the use of embedded double quotes, thus: "*This* sentence, namely, '*This* sentence, namely, "*This* sentence is false," is false,' is false." And so on ad infinitum. Basic considerations here are that (1) all statements must be regarded as stating something intelligible *before* they can even be analyzed for reference; and (2) demonstrative pronouns or adjectives and other ostensive words cannot properly be utilized to refer to the sentence or clause in which they are immediately contained, without overextending their referential capacities ("this statement is true" properly applies to some other statement, only ambiguously to itself); and (3) the overextensions in question become clearly highlighted in attempts at *contradictory* self-reference such as the liar paradox.

To some, it seems that a satisfactory way of representing the liar paradox would be to use Quine's quotation-method " 'Contains a falsehood' contains a falsehood." But here again grammar enters in, because the conventions of speech seem to require that we add "this" or "this sentence" before the first instance of "contains," and this addition would bring us back to a more recognizable and more disturbing form of the liar paradox.

As regards the well-known paradox of the Barber of Seville, who shaves all and only those who do not shave themselves: when the inevitable question about whether he shaves himself arises, even proper formulation of the paradoxical question is inhibited by grammar and usage. For even if we ignore the fact that a barber is by definition someone who shaves someone else, the "all *those*" shaven by the Barber seems to refer by linguistic convention to others *besides* the Barber. Children and women are excluded by implication, and oneself is neither included nor excluded. A clarification of the strange-sounding formulation might be possible if we test it by reference to an empirical case in which it might conceivably be applicable: There is, let us say, an amateur barber in Seville who donates his time to shaving all and only those who do not shave themselves, i.e., those who are unable or unwilling to shave themselves, but willing to be shaved, e.g., handicapped people and indolent youth. It is probable that he also shaves himself; but it is also possible that his neighbor, who is a retired barber, shaves himself and also the "Barber of Seville." If one wanted to reduce ambiguity, "Man of Seville" could be substituted for "Barber of Seville," and "all adult males, not including himself" could replace "all those." But then the paradox would disappear. (I am tempted at this point to introduce a second-order paradox about the philosopher who solved paradoxes for all and only those who could not solve paradoxes for themselves. Does he solve paradoxes for himself? If so, does he solve only first-order paradoxes, or does he also solve this second-order paradox?)

Logical proofs have of course been offered to corroborate the fact that the subject in the Barber paradox cannot be assumed to be in the same set as the people of Seville whom he shaves; but it would seem that at least those who agreed to the correspondence between the symbolic logical formulations and the ordinary language translation of the symbols would be able to come to a conclusion on a purely *grammatical* basis that the question as to whether or not the Barber shaves himself does not even arise, but is a pseudo-problem, in the context of the actually given formulation of this "paradox."

One must entertain analogous doubts about the alleged verbal expressibility of Gödel's Incompleteness Theorem in the system of natural numbers, considered by some to be a sophisticated modern parallel to the liar paradox, insofar as (they claim) it is a formula from number theory geared to proving that it is outside the ambit of the proof-capabilities of its own system. Findlay offers basically a two-step translation of Gödel's theorem into English,[1] which can be paraphrased as follows:

> 1. Let $F$ = "We cannot prove the statement which is arrived at by substituting for the variable in the statement-form $Y$ the name of the statement-form in question."

2. Let $G$ = "We cannot prove the statement which is arrived at by substituting for the variable in the statement-form $F$ the name of the statement-form in question." Then make the substitution called for in $G$ by replacing the variable $Y$ in $F$ with the name of the statement-form in question, which (says Findlay) is $F$ itself.

It is a good thing that Findlay informs us that the name of the statement-form "in question" is $F$, because grammatically speaking it is not absolutely clear that "the name of the statement-form in question" *has* to refer to $F$. And so, if this be a valid English translation, it does not seem to clearly contain the paradox that we suppose to be there. The translation, of course, might be invalid, and Gödel's theorem is presumably less troublesome than the liar paradox in its pure mathematical symbolism where it is untrammeled by grammatical reference-problems and propositional conceptions of "truth."

Various escapes have been offered by philosophers to the befuddled mind in the face of such paradoxes—including Ryle's theory of categories, Russell's theory of types, Tarski's distinction between physical-object language and various meta-languages, and von Neumann's class-set distinction. But some disgruntled philosophers are still not satisfied, and the "escapes" remain controversial. Quine objects to Russell's solution insofar as it gives rise to an infinite series of "universal" classes, each corresponding to higher and higher types.[2] Eric Toms challenges the characterization of Ryle's theory as a "linguistic" approach on the grounds that "a generalization *from* actual linguistic usage [aside from linguistic rules] obviously cannot be used as a principle for *correcting* actual linguistic usage."[3] Toms also argues that Ushenko's refutation of the liar paradox on the grounds of "meaninglessness" is inconclusive—in spite of some mistakes made by Ushenko's critics regarding the type-token distinction.[4] And Max Black assails the theory-of-types approach in general because it invalidly assumes that $\phi x$ is meaningful only if $x$ does not have the value $\phi$, or anything involving $\phi$, so that self-reference becomes impossible.

P. E. B. Jourdain and Karl Popper, on the other hand, have
tried to make the liar paradox disappear of its own accord by
dividing it into two statements which refer to each other. (In
Popper's version, [1] "The next assertion I am going to make is
a true one"; [2] "The last assertion I made was untrue.") Such
bisected versions help to highlight the ineluctable tendency
(discussed above) of demonstrative and ostensive terms to refer
outward to antecedents or referents rather than to the sentence or
clause in which they are immediately contained; but in the
process of bisection, they also seem to substitute mere contradiction for the element of *vicious circularity* and for the concomitant appearance of self-reference that seems to be an essential ingredient of the liar paradox and its bona fide variations. It
is interesting to note that when Gödel's theorem was translated
by Findlay into the ordinary-language formulation reproduced
above, Findlay found it necessary to replace the single theorem
with two statements referring to each other, as Popper had to do
with the liar paradox.

The "set-theoretical" paradoxes, some steps removed from
ordinary language and grammar, seem to result from the natural
limitations of our logical categories and generalizations. Specifically, they raise the question: How can a general set (e.g.,
the set of all sets with multiple members) encompass itself-*as-
general?* For it seems that if $s$ is a general set and encompasses
"itself," the resultant self-encompassing set, $s_1$, is related to $s$
now as general to particular (or more general to less general),
and thus is now not much more "self-encompassing" than a
box whose outer surface encompasses its inner surface. Russell's type-theory, which was calculated to obviate set-theoretic
paradoxes by erecting a rigid hierarchy of sets devised to ensure
that no set is—or can be—a member of itself, seems to be
simply a recognition of an already-existent situation in logic.
But Russell's attempt to make a logical rule about an already-
implicit logical rule seems to have carried him beyond the

boundaries of logic, as Black and Ushenko, in their divergent critiques of the theory of types, both converged in alleging.

If one were to try to make a *rule* about paradox-*solutions* such as Russell's theory of types, which is already a logical rule about logical rules, he would by continuing this operation find himself in another category of paradox, the "paradoxes of infinity" (which involve an infinite regress). Zeno's "Achilles" paradox, the Lewis Carroll paradox of an infinity of proof-implications, Bradley's paradox of relations, and Aristotle's famous "third man" argument against Plato also purportedly belong to this same category. The paradoxes of infinity have been taken quite seriously by Alan White, who proposed his "shooting-gallery" solution to Zeno's Achilles,[5] by Russell, who in *Principia Mathematica* proposed a distinction between rules of inference and hypothetical propositions to obviate the Lewis Carroll paradox, and by Toms, who refutes the same paradox on the grounds that the regress of inferences is caused by a misunderstanding of the finality of substitution and specification in formal logic.[6] But one may with reason entertain some doubts as to whether such "paradoxes of infinity" (aside from the question of their validity) are really entitled to be designated "paradoxes" at all. Something seems to be missing. Yes, they do illustrate limits. Just as the set-theoretic paradoxes illustrate the limits of the logical processes of abstraction and generalization, so also do the paradoxes of infinity illustrate the limits on our power of demonstrating and justifying relationships—whether it is a question of spatial relationships (Zeno's Achilles), the relationships between ideas (Bradley's paradox), or the relationships between logical antecedents and consequents (Carroll's paradox). But there is only a minimum of self-reference involved, as a particular set of relations seems to broaden or deepen itself into an infinity of relations. And, most important, there is no intrinsic element of *contradiction* in the paradoxes of infinity. There is a species of extrinsic contradiction, insofar as these paradoxes come into opposition with our normal expectations and ways of thought. And this entitles them to the designation, "paradox," in the wide sense (in the same sense that, e.g., something that happens contrary to the opinion or expectations of everyone might be considered "paradoxical"). But for paradox in the strict sense, as even the dictionary indicates, some type of contradictory state of affairs or situation of opposition must be expressed in the very words used. And so both self-reference and contradiction seem to be minimal in the paradoxes of infinity.

Grelling's paradoxical question—"Is 'heterological' heterological?"—is an interesting attempt to manifest both self-reference and contradiction, but it is also grammatically engendered. It can be clarified, if not solved, on the grammatical level by attention to the use of quotation marks around a word, which renders that word so different from the same word without quotation marks that, for example, a strict grammarian would never even consider the possibility that " 'heterological' " could be homological to "heterological." Nevertheless, it comes perhaps as close as any of the paradoxes to illustrating in a concise and intuitive way the basic thrust of paradox toward the use of words that *almost* seem to bend back upon themselves and seize upon some basic contradiction at their core.

But we all know—don't we?—that neither words nor series of words in sentences *can* bend back upon themselves in this way. Only consciousnesses can do that. Even if words *could* be enabled to approximate the conscious human movements of self-consciousness, it has seemed important, and probably is important for clarity, that we keep our everyday language and logic relatively free from self-reference. At least this seems to be the reasoning and motivation of the multitude of philosophers from the time of Aristotle until the present who have done their best to combat paradox or the possibility of paradoxical outcomes or solutions.

But although many philosophers have made noble efforts to combat or minimize paradoxical self-reference and self-contradiction, success continually escapes them. Graham Priest contends that all the solutions that have been offered for semantical and logical-syntactical paradoxes so far have been mere "ad hoc," aspirinlike remedies, since they give no reason for rejecting faulty premise(s) except that the premise(s) block the "acceptable" solution.[7] Should this be a cause for dismay? Eric Toms not only challenges the solutions to the paradoxes but challenges the assumption that the paradoxes are a problem. In Toms's logical-ontological analyses, paradox is portrayed as an "overnecessitated" result of some logical inferences—a result which is not embarrassing but is a positive and progressive development. Toms's negative-reflective paradox—"There are no negative facts"[8]—bears obvious similarities to the liar paradox, since if the statement is true, then the statement itself exists as at least one negative fact and falsifies itself. It helps show that negation and contradictions are not just logical operations sheltered from reality, but have continual ontological implications: negative facts do exist. The negative-reflexive paradox (Toms maintains) is thus not just a challenge to be overcome with further advances in logical theory, but an indication that logic in its constitutional inhibition of paradoxes is incomplete in its ability to express truths, some, and perhaps many, of which are paradoxical in nature.

Toms suggests[9] that paradoxes are a problem only for orthodox logic, not for ordinary languages (physical-object language, electron language, sense-data language, etc.) which are based in reality and make or assume the appropriate distinctions (he assumes that such ordinary languages have the grammatical capacity to represent adequately paradoxical situations). Toms is joined in his contentions by a few other philosophers, notably Stéphane Lupasco[10] and George Melhuish,[11] both of whom, although basing their arguments for a paradoxical logic primarily on logico-metaphysical considerations, make no secret of the fact that they receive both strong motivation, and intellectual support, from contemporary developments in mathematics and physics for adopting the positions they do adopt. Before going on to further logical and philosophical aspects of this question, let us take a look at some of these developments in other spheres which seem to supply at least an impetus for reexamining the assumptions, procedures, and/or scope of traditional nonparadoxical logic.

## Mathematics, Science, and Paradox

As indicated above[12], Gödel's Incompleteness Theorem bears an interesting resemblance to the liar's paradox. But since it involves a statement from within a strong system about the system as a whole, it goes beyond the mere undecidability of the liar-type paradoxes to sweeping implications regarding system-limitations. It demonstrates that the very axioms which are meant to assure the systematic consistency of number theory lead, by a kind of overkill, to an ironical incompleteness. Predicate calculus, not pretending to such strength and consistency, ends up as apparently more complete. At least, there is no way to demonstrate *its* incompleteness in a single, neat formula in Gödelian fashion. But it certainly cannot encompass paradoxes. And this would be an incompleteness of sorts, unless one summarily dismisses all paradoxes as nonsensical. However, as I hope to show in some of the sections that follow, the logical and semantical paradoxes are easier to dismiss as nonsensical than literary, religious, and philosophical paradoxes.

Variations of Gödel's theorem and various applications to computers have been produced by Church, Turing, Tarski, and others. Lucas has suggested[13] that Gödel's Theorem applied to artificial intelligence systems shows that these systems are essentially and immutably inferior to the human mind, since even the most advanced computer cannot formulate the Incompleteness Theorem about its own system. To formulate this theorem requires one in some sense to stand outside the material existence and limitations of his own system—something that presumably no machine can do. Even if a machine were pro-

grammed by some human operator to produce successive Gödelian formulae ad infinitum, the machine (to speak anthropo-
morphically) would not have the slightest awareness of the
incompleteness of its total system, while a human operator who
was cognizant of the finite specifications leading to the "Gödelizing" operations *would* be aware of the incompleteness,
and give formal expression to this awareness by the appropriate
Gödelian formula. However, it is obvious that if the Gödelizing
operations became too complex, even the most resourceful
human being would find it impossible to comprehend the status
of their incompleteness and give expression to them in mathematical G-formulae. And so it seems the most Lucas could
maintain is that when minds and machines carry out operations
of similar complexity there is an element of awareness in minds
that cannot be discerned in machines; and that it is the mind's
conviction of incompleteness that enables the operator to pro-
gram the computer to prove that incompleteness in the first
place. This mode of argumentation is, of course, simply a
contemporary variation on the traditional spiritualist-materialist
controversy as to whether the mind is reducible to the brain and
neural operations or in some fashion stands above its corporeal
"instruments" in a soulish way. Lucas's argument, besides
reflecting that old controversy, adds the interesting suggestion
that our awareness of the incompleteness of the systems we
construct may be a, or perhaps *the,* basic human characteristic.

Quantum physicists, unlike mathematicians, are not just re-
signed to the existence of paradoxes—they welcome and perpetuate hypotheses that seem paradoxical from the vantage
point of ordinary observation and even Newtonian physics. A
fundamental paradox of quantum physics, which goes against
our ordinary ideas of objectivity, is presented in the "Copen-
hagen Interpretation" of Bohr and Heisenberg, which states
that an observing system (i.e., the instrumentation and equipment used and the human observers) alters the observed system
(e.g., atomic particles), so that "objective reality" is always
heavily influenced by our subjective interpretive procedures

and devices. It is in accord with this interpretation that Heisenberg tells us that the certainty produced by the "observing system" about position (or time) in subatomic particle physics would generate uncertainty in the measurement of momentum (or energy), and vice versa. Einstein and other physicists have considered such statements "paradoxical" in the pejorative sense of that term—i.e., highly suspicious because conflicting with the sort of predictability they had considered essential to the physical sciences. However, since the late 1930s quantum mechanics, whose statistical predictions have proved impeccable, has been almost universally accepted; and its possible independence of Newtonian ideas of ordinary "local" causality was dramatically demonstrated in 1964, when Bell's theorem (confirmed experimentally in 1972) hypothesized a type of connection between the horizontal and vertical polarization of spatially separate particles that seems to bypass all the traditional concepts of causal connections in space.

In contemporary microphysical experiments and analyses, paradoxical events take place as a matter of course: in accord with Bohr's complementarity principle, the same physical reality may be interpreted as either a particle or a wave at different times or from different points of view; causes (as depicted by Feynman diagrams) are charted as coming after their effects; a positron traveling forward in time is equated to an electron traveling backwards in time; in the "vacuum diagrams" instantaneous reactions come out of nothingness and disappear; according to the time-reversal principle, a process must be reversible in time in order to be possible; entities like photons— described by Heisenberg as "in the middle" between possibility and reality—are taken for granted; the smallest particles are destructible in collision experiments but indestructible insofar as they are reconstituted by the energy generated in the collision; matter can be treated as a continuous field or as discontinuous particles; and, in general, electrons, protons, neutrons, photons, and other particles seem to be implicated in one another in much the same way that opposites and contradictions are mutually implicated in paradoxes. And so it is not surprising that the very existence of quantum physics is taken by some as one of the chief corroborations from the contemporary world of science that a paradoxical worldview is no longer to be avoided as absurd or unsophisticated.

If quantum physics had to do with first-order (physical) realities, in the way that Newtonian physics has to do, such conclusions would seem to be warranted. Erwin Schrödinger originally interpreted electrons and other microcosmic objects as material waves, but Max Born in 1926 argued that the Schrödinger "waves" are really waves of probability, i.e., wave-functions resulting from statistical calculations. Quantum physics would seem thus to be dealing primarily with second-order realities (probabilistic interpretations of the physical world). The quantum physicist does not speak (unless he forgets himself momentarily) about the precise, actual momentum of this or that particle, or of the factual existence of virtual particles created from a photon; rather, he speaks of the wave-functions on his graph-making equipment and the probabilities of particle momentum, emission of virtual particles, etc., that are predicted as a result of his calculations from these wave-functions. He has nothing directly to do with actually existent particles or waves (if they do exist) but with statistical probabilities that such-and-such an experiment with his particle accelerator will yield evidence regarding the status of particles, waves, etc. Possibly, as Werner Heisenberg hypothesized, the quantum physicist is dealing with intermediate realities—something analogous to Aristotle's principle of "potency"; or possibly, as John von Neumann suggested, we might characterize the findings of quantum physics as a "logical calculus," affected by the Uncertainty Principle, and concerned specifically with the relation between wave-functions and the properties of physical systems. In any case, we clearly cannot utilize quantum physics as a springboard to leap facilely to the conclusion that "reality is paradoxical," although we can at the minimum point to it as support for the hypothesis that subatomic reality subjected to mental examination and our measuring instruments yields paradoxical second-order results.

George Melhuish, concerned with applying Lupasco's ground-breaking work in paradoxical logic to the physical world, does seem to lapse occasionally into first-order language about the findings of quantum physics, speaking, for example, of electrons no longer being subject to traditional forms of causation[14] and the inapplicability of Cartesian coordinates to the physical world;[15] but for the most part he portrays the entities of quantum mechanics as a replacement of the stable actualities of Newtonian physics with the old Aristotelian idea of potentiality, as an intermediate state between being and nothingness. Melhuish also takes pains to remind us that Heisenberg's Uncertainty Principle applies not just to the submicroscopic world but to the cosmos at large. And he suggests that the major deficiency of traditional logic in handling the macroscopic world is in dealing with change. Ordinary logic, he says, because of its very nature and presuppositions, must end up with a static view of the world and a staticization of change. And so, rather than refuting Zeno's ''Achilles'' paradox, Melhuish uses it as a kind of object-lesson to illustrate the deep-rooted and almost *a priori* tendency of traditional logic to consider all change embarrassingly ''paradoxical'' insofar as it unites opposite or contradictory states in an entity.[16]

## *Logico-Philosophical Considerations*

Gödel's Incompleteness Theorem, quantum events, the Uncertainty Principle, etc., can supply no more than indirect evidence of some important shortcomings in traditional nonparadoxical logic. For more direct evidence, we have to examine the three foundational pillars of that logic—the laws of identity, contradiction, and excluded middle. Hegel, who maintained that these principles were applicable only to an intermediate stage of thinking, was one of the first modern thinkers to challenge all three:

The maxim of Identity reads: Everything is identical with itself, A = A: and negatively, A cannot at the same time be A and not A. This maxim, instead of being a true law of thought, is nothing but the law of abstract understanding. The propositional form itself contradicts it: for a proposition always promises a distinction between subject and predicate.[17]

A notion which possesses neither or both of two mutually contradictory marks, e.g. a quadrangular circle, is held to be logically false. Now though a multiangular circle and a rectilineal arc no less contradict this maxim, geometers never hesitate to treat the circle as a polygon with rectilineal sides.[18]

The Maxim of Excluded Middle is the maxim of the definite understanding, which would fain avoid contradiction, but in so doing falls into it. A must be either +A or −A, it says. It virtually declares in these words a third [neutral] A which is neither + nor −, and which at the same time is yet invested with + and − characters.

Dogmatism consists in the tenacity which draws a hard and fast line between certain terms and others opposite to them. We may see this clearly in the strict "Either-or": for instance, the world is either finite or infinite; but one of these two it must be. The contrary of this rigidity is the characteristic of all Speculative truth. . . . The soul is neither finite only, nor infinite only; it is really the one just as much as the other, and in that way neither the one nor the other. . . . We say of sensible things, that they are changeable: that is, they *are*, but it is equally true that they are *not*.[19]

Since Hegel's time, specific challenges to the three logical laws have also come from other sectors.

*Identity:* Wittgenstein in his *Tractatus*[20] suggests that there is something wrong with the so-called analytical truth, *A = A*. If indeed A is simply equal to A, why bother to say anything about it? In order to avoid such useless tautologies, Wittgenstein proposes, with tongue-in-cheek, that we content ourselves with saying, A = ?. The result of such considerations in Aristotelian syllogistic logic is the so-called "paradox of judgment": "S is P" can only be meaningful if S and P are different; but then "S = P" is false. The ordinary means for establishing a relation of syllogistic identity-in-difference is the utilization of a "middle term." But this solution relies on the fact that the middle term is, in a sense, *reflexive*,[21] i.e., both relates and is the term being related, even though logic, which militates against propositional self-reference, certainly also militates against a single term being self-referential, as is indicated by the Lewis Carroll paradox. In recognition of the fact that relationships of "identity" entail difference, when Hegel on certain occasions wanted to give a concrete example of the mediations of dialectic, he pointed for elucidation to the standard Aristotelian syllogism, in which the subject, via a middle term, is at one and the same time different from the predicate and identical with the predicate. And when we proceed beyond A = A and S is P to the p ↔ p of formal logic, we must still face the question raised by Lewis Carroll's paradox: If the conclusion doesn't say something different from the premises, it is not worth saying; but, when we do say something different, how do we ever get beyond the premises to the conclusion which differs from it?

*Noncontradiction:* The most conservative challenge to the hegemony of the law of noncontradiction (NC) comes from Nicholas Rescher, who, unlike Toms, maintains a rigid distinction between thought and mundane reality, a distinction which enables him to theorize about inconsistent worlds in which NC does not hold.[22] If we reason about inconsistent worlds, says Rescher, our *thought* can still be consistent. In effect, Rescher handles contradictions and also paradoxes in the way that the Everet-Wheeler hypothesis handles the unorthodox suppositions of quantum physics: by positing other worlds—contradictory worlds—which serve to separate contradictory elements that would be embarrassing and unmanageable if they referred to our present world. Rescher's *Logic of Inconsistency* results in overdetermined disjunction-worlds in which $[P]_{w_1} \cup_{w_2} = +$ iff $[P]_{w_1} = +$ or $[P]_{w_2} = +$ ("the proposition $P$ obtains in the disjunction-worlds if and only if it obtains either in world #1 or in world #2"). But even in Rescher's "overdetermined" worlds, there are both inconsistent types of inconsistencies and consistent types (a result which is itself a logical and possibly a logico-philosophical paradox). And in general, Rescher insists that his conclusions completely accord with the rules of classical formal logic.

But even with regard to our present and actual world, we might ask whether the law of contradiction ever finds a "pure" application. If it does, then a pencil cannot be both round and not-round, a hermaphrodite cannot be both male and nonmale, an American traitor cannot be both American and non-American, a moral choice cannot be both necessitated and not-necessitated, an ambivert cannot be both an extrovert and a nonextrovert, and so on. The Aristotelian qualification, "in different respects," does not really solve the logical predicament here, because "in different respects" does not just weaken the "non-" or "not-" but absolutely contradicts the thrust of the principle of contradiction, which was devised to prevent any coexistence of incompatible predicates. If, for example, we were to try to say that Socrates is mortal in certain respects and immortal in other respects, we could do so only by splitting up Socrates so severely as to strike a fatal blow to his personal unity. If we were to try to salvage this situation by modifying our contention to the mere contention that Socrates' body is mortal while his soul is immortal, we would solve the contradiction only to raise a new question and another potential contradiction: namely, which one is Socrates? his body or soul? (Plato, by equating Socrates with his soul, avoided this sort of question; but Aristotle's mortal/immortal, body/soul human composite broached the question anew.) One who accepts NC in its rigor, although he may be unconscious of the fact, has a "vested interest" in seeing and portraying the world as black and white—overlooking any shades of gray, which would inevitably involve us in "paradoxes." Going beyond such intuitive considerations, Toms argues[23] that since the Rule of Inference, $\sim p \vee q, p, \therefore q$ *presupposes* the law of NC, it is invalid to "prove" NC, i.e., to *infer* it, as is the convention, at a late stage of the propositional calculus, at which NC is already accepted and presupposed and utilized in proofs. The essence of NC, says Toms, is $p \leftrightarrow \sim\sim p$. But $\sim\sim p$ cannot be inferred either by *Modus ponens* or by intuition. Toms also argues that logical negation comes into conflict with the "paradox of negation" (PN). While a negation of $p$ usually is interpreted as implying nothing about the existence of $p$, PN implies that the negation of $p$ cannot be made unless there *is* some positive fact $p$. One cannot, for example, deny the existence of unicorns unless unicorns exist as a fact to be denied. And one who, in the face of such considerations, would still insist that there are no negative facts would necessarily find himself in the throes of the negative-reflexive paradox, according to which his denial, as a second-order negative fact, would nullify the denial he is trying to make on the first-order level.

*Excluded middle:* Toms notes that although the other two logical laws are reducible to the law of excluded middle (EM), EM itself is neither analytic nor synthetic, and could not even be called "tautological" or "trivial," since the presence or absence of tautology or triviality is by reduction determined with *reference to* EM. Presumably, Toms conjectures, EM is based on some nonconceptualizable, nonspeculative, nonmetaphysical intuition. But this contradicts the logical empiricist's restriction of intuition to sensible awareness and/or verbal awareness (of tautologies). And this intuition causes us to set up artificial and unreal dichotomies between male and nonmale, extrovert and introvert, etc., although in slightly different form than the dichotomies resulting from NC.

Melhuish offers the traditional problem of creation "ex nihilo" as an example of a metaphysical problem resulting from the dichotomizations of EM:

> In considering the problem of creation *ex nihilo*, we are forced to maintain an *actual* potentiality between noth-

ing and something (we cannot do less), and this implies an active correspondence between the one state and the other. Yet if there is any correspondence whatsoever between nothing and something, then there must always have been such a correspondence. . . . We cannot decree that what there is came from nothing since the sheer unpotentiality of such a nothing would render all existence impossible.[24]

Leslie Armour, arguing that it is impossible to focus on any positive fact without indicating by implication its negative counterfacts, seconds Toms's contention, offering numerous examples of the deficiency of EM.[25] First-order examples would be the following: "Either this is a butterfly or this is not a butterfly." (What about the egg, the chrysalis, etc.?) Or: "Either what I am talking about is a part of God or what I am talking about is not a part of God." (Theologians who talk about qualities predicated of God *per eminentiam* would not be able to agree with this disjunction.) Armour also points to the second-order proposition which paraphrases EM—"Either $P$ refers to $Q$ or $P$ does not refer to $Q$"—as the primordial and paradigmatic example of the insufficiency of EM, since if $P$ does not refer to $Q$, it does refer in a negative way to $Q$ by excluding it.

In addition to these three apparent foundational weaknesses in formal logic, one might mention the more widely recognized though still debated weakness with regard to the use of the universal quantifier "all" in predicate logic, often with minimal justification from questionable laws of induction.

Even if we agree with some or all of the above challenges to traditional logic, we must be careful not to "throw out the baby with the bathwater" by construing these challenges as adequate grounds for extolling a nontraditional, "dialectical" (or "paradoxical" or "nonselective") logic to such an extent that ordinary logic is relegated to a minor or subservient role. Melhuish, although he admits that traditional "selective" logic presents us with "half the truth," is so earnest in his apologetic for a paradoxical logic that it is hard to see how and where the traditional logic would fit in, if his proposals were adopted.

On the other hand, as Thomas Kuhn has shown with regard to scientific paradigms,[26] there is an inveterate tendency among established scholars to resist acceptance of the results of investigation when these come into conflict with the prevailing paradigms. If this is true of the laws of science, which are supposedly most responsive to empirical input, we may suppose that it also applies to logic, which has been considerably distanced from whatever empirical roots it may have had. And indeed Quine and other staunch supporters of the importance and centrality of our logical laws have pointed out the danger of similar conservative tendencies among philosophers and logicians. Widespread conservatism in logic would be a major obstacle to even a strongly substantiated dialectical logic.

To sum up this series of ''external considerations'': Grammar seems to be even more successful in preventing self-reference (affirmative or negative) than formal logic, or at least constitutes an ''advance guard'' against self-reference. Ordinary language and its grammar, however, possibly aiming at completeness more than consistency, seem to have a much greater tolerance of the sorts of non-self-referential apparent contradictions that we often designate as ''paradoxes.'' At the present time quantum physics would seem to be a prime example of the ability of ordinary language (as applied to microphysical events) to tolerate such ''inconsistencies,'' in apparent disregard of logical laws; but some paradoxes of quantum physics may be only *apparent* paradoxes, i.e., not mere ''apparent contradictions,'' but true contradictions, susceptible to solution through further theoretical advances. If number theory by means of Gödel's theorem is indeed more successful in presenting a true and unassailable *quasi*-self-referential and *quasi*-self-negating paradox than predicate logic, this may be so because the Incompleteness Theorem restricts itself by design to the very limited domain of number theory, where the correspondence of ideas with empirical reality in the larger sense is not of the utmost importance. The constant disputes as to logic's ability or inability to handle the multitude of standard paradoxes seems to rise from a schizophrenic tendency on the part of logic to (1) be applicable to all of reality, and thus complete; and (2) to be rigidly consistent as a formal system, second only to mathematics, and thus impervious to any of the "contradictions" which might pop up in reality—leading some logicians even to claims about logic's independence from reality. Rising above such disputes, one suspects that logical and semantic paradoxes are only apparent paradoxes, i.e., not mere "apparent" self-contradictions but real contradictions to be avoided.

One reaction against perceived deficiencies in logic may be to investigate and/or develop an unorthodox, "dialectical" logic, more capable of dealing with, e.g., the convergence of opposite ideas, interpretations, or conclusions, possibly combined with nonvicious self-reference. We turn in chapter 2 to consider the grounds or possible grounds for such a dialectical logic; and the most convenient place to begin such a consideration is with a reexamination of the phenomenological origins of traditional logic.

# 2

# Self-Consciousness and the Origins of Dialectic

I distinguish myself from myself, and in doing so I am directly aware that what is distinguished from myself is not different [from me]. I, the selfsame being, repel myself from myself; but what is posited as distinct from me, or as unlike me, is immediately, in being so distinguished, not a distinction for me. . . . Consciousness of an "other," of an object in general, is itself necessarily *self-consciousness*, a reflectedness-into-self, consciousness of itself in its otherness.
—Hegel, *The Phenomenology of Spirit*, Introduction

## *Ordinary Logic and the Subject/Object Distinction*

The phenomenological experience most fundamental to the emergence of traditional logic would seem to be the experience of the subject-object (S/O) distinction. The S/O distinction is taken for granted so thoroughly by us that we may easily forget that it is not a standard operation from the time of birth in human beings. Psychologists, sociologists, and cultural anthropologists have pointed out that the orientation toward this distinction as we know it (with a clear and sharp differentiation of external reality from consciousness, as a subjectivity separate from the world "out there") has only gradually emerged in the human race as a whole, has only "come into its own" since the Renaissance and Enlightenment, and in some parts of the world (e.g., where animism prevails) is still only latent. With regard to the individual human being, developmental psychologists tell us that, on the average, the human infant only comes to make a definite and adequate distinction between the ego and objects in the external world during the last half of the first twelve months of life. The ability to make the S/O distinction confers on its possessor certain advantages which are indubitably relevant to the development and effective application of traditional logic:

1. It makes possible the consciousness of stable objects with stable predicates. Prior to the advent of the S/O distinction, the infant or the cultural primitive does not really recognize objects as external to, and independent from, his own ego; as something that can perdure even when he takes no notice of it; or as a stable substratum for stable predicates to be assigned in accord with the laws of logic and the demands of reality.

2. It conditions "objective" interpretations of reality, based purely on the facts and the laws of logical inference. Needless to say, one must resolutely differentiate everything of psychical origin from external being, if he is to avoid "subjective" interpretations, and the primordial S/O distinction is a *sine qua non* for such differentiations.

3. As a kind of anticurrent to objectivity of the empirical sort, the S/O distinction may also be said to be responsible for engendering a sense of freedom and power in formulating distinctions, criteria, ideas, and ideals in seeming independence of the external world—tendencies which reach their zenith in stoicism, skepticism, solipsism, and the pursuit of the "a priori" associated with idealism. However, if, like Kant, we consider conformity-to-our-ideas a necessary condition for objectivity, these same tendencies in combination with logic may be taken as conducive to objectivity, albeit objectivity of a Kantian sort ("objective" just insofar as it is in conformity with our logic and concepts).

4. The S/O distinction is also foundational to the making of clear distinctions, not only between the subject-consciousness and its external objects, but also between the inner nature of objects and their appearance-to-us, between two or more objects which we differentiate from ourselves in different ways or at different times, and between the so-called "subject" of a proposition (which ironically refers to some object or objectified consciousness) and the proposition's predicate (which, again ironically, designates the attributes which we subjectively recognize in the object in question).

5. Finally, the S/O distinction contributes to clear-cut negations: If we consider the sort of objections that have been discussed above against NC and EM, we might be persuaded that both the origin of these principles and the problems we have with them can be traced in large part to the S/O distinction. Why is it that we presuppose negation in some absolute sense, and the result of such negation to be absolute nothingness (which everyone admits to be a thoroughly incomprehensible idea)? Is it not because the S/O distinction itself requires our objects to be absolutely "other"? It would not do, after all, for us to be merging ourselves with our objects or for our objects to be intertwining themselves with our psyche, if we want to be credited with scientific or even objective discourse and attitudes at all. Even if we were thus merged and intertwined, it would behoove us not only to distance but to distinguish and sunder ourselves from something "out there," if we wanted to talk about it at all.

Thus, to sum up, the S/O distinction seems to be the foundation for a long series of pivotal distinctions and negations that, either implicitly or in the explicit form of logical rules, help us to avoid a constant and intractable inrush of ambiguities—such as would arise when Socrates is neither mortal nor immortal, John is neither present nor absent, etc.

But, granted that the S/O distinction is a great boon to the banishment of ambiguities, it itself is not completely clear. If it were impeccably clear, it would seem we should have little difficulty in answering a simple question like "where does the subject end, and the object begin, or vice versa?'' But it is even difficult to formulate the question precisely, since ''end'' and ''begin'' belong primarily to object-language and its subdivision, space-language; so that we are straining the tolerances of logic from the outset in even asking the question. However, if we try to bypass semantical problems for the moment and get at the intent of the question, which most of us can readily understand, the very attempt at an answer helps illustrate the ambiguity of that S/O distinction that we take so readily for granted: Do we want to say, with Freud, that the peripheries of the ego are at the outer surfaces of the skin, and everything beyond is the nonego? Or would we prefer with some of the materialist school to say that consciousness for all practical purposes resides in the neurons or gray matter, while everything else is nonconscious matter? Or would we prefer to say, after the manner of some phenomenologists, that otherness resides just beyond ''the horizons'' of our perceptions and/or conceptualizations? If we can never be exact about the precise locus for the S/O distinction, we can harbor proportionally less hope of being exact about all the manifold subsidiary distinctions that seem to hinge directly or indirectly on that primordial distinction.

It is in the light of this obscurely rooted but strongly affirmed S/O distinction that *self-reference* becomes problematical and leads, or seems to lead, to logical, semantical, or grammatical paradoxes. For our language and logic, constitutionally adapted to preserving the S/O distinction, are ill-equipped to convey the bending-back-upon-self that seems to be involved in self-reference. And one who is interested in preserving the integrity and clarity of our language systems may even argue convincingly that linguistic self-reference has a potential for self-destruction that is worrisome and must be checked. The ancient symbol of the snake destroying itself by swallowing its own tail comes to mind. The crusader against paradoxes is no doubt intent on keeping language or logic from swallowing itself, so to speak. But since not only self-reference but also self-contradiction seem to be essential to the most formidable logical and semantic paradoxes the consummate crusader will be possibly lenient with mere self-references as in the "paradoxes of infinity," and focus his efforts on the aforesaid apparent combinations of self-reference with self-*contradiction*.

But if our crusader were successful in his onslaught, would he really be performing a worthwhile service for philosophy and logic? It seems that the interdiction of self-reference and self-contradiction is a direct result of those rules of logic and grammar that are geared to protecting a S/O distinction which falls short of being an absolute and unquestionable fact or value (the distinction between fact and value being another exemplification of the S/O distinction itself). It is interesting that Toms[1] proposes self-reference or self-reflection in the universe as a whole as a possible *solution* for Bradley's paradox. Is it conceivable that self-reference is not only a cause but also (and possibly on a grand scale) the solution of the "problem" of paradox (leading us to a kind of ultimate second-order paradox)?

## Reflection and Dialectic

I would suggest (or, more precisely, reemphasize a suggestion made by Hegel) that the basic phenomenological condition germane to logic is not the S/O distinction, but consciousness in a more general sense.[2] The subject-object distinction is only one, albeit a major, aspect of our experience of consciousness. The experience of *self*-consciousness and reflection is equal in importance to the experience of the S/O distinction. And it is precisely this reflective or self-referential aspect of consciousness that ordinary logic cannot easily handle. Perhaps this inability is not just coincidental. For self-consciousness *is* that class which is a member of itself (so troublesome to Russell); it *is* an instance of that "self-thinking thought" that Aristotle took pains to relegate to a sphere beyond mundane species and genera. It might be profitable for us to look for some clues to an understanding of paradox in self-consciousness itself, which seems to be the source not only for our idea of self-reference (whether or not this idea can be expressed in ordinary logic and language), but also for our idea of a viable (paradoxical) type of contradiction:

Self-consciousness engenders self-reference and paradox and is perhaps the most fundamental of all paradoxes. Primordially, self-consciousness is a fusion of subject and object, such that the conscious subject makes itself into its own object or, conversely, a particular type of object in the world grasps itself subjectively. Secondarily, and contingent upon this primordial fusion, self-consciousness makes possible a fusion of mental entities which would be judged merely contradictory by the standards of ordinary logic—namely:

1. *Unity (identity) and difference:* Self-consciousness is a two-in-one. It requires the splitting up of a single consciousness into the knowing side and the known side; but the known and the knower are patently identical. The state of self-consciousness might best be described in the Hegelian mode, as an identity *of* identity *and* difference, in which the overarching identity is a second-order identity, an $identity_2$, while the subsumed identity is an $identity_1$. Note that the $identity_1$, which is contrasted with difference, is *different from* the $identity_2$, which brings $identity_1$ and difference together. In other words, self-consciousness is not *just* a unity of its subjective and objective aspects, but a unity-in-difference of its unification of these aspects and its differentiation of them. This overarching $identity_2$, which, unlike $identity_1$, does not stand apart as something different from difference, seems to be the basis for the tendency of consciousness to formulate paradoxes—a tendency concerned, of course, with bringing together opposites in such a way that they are no longer opposite in their former and univocal sense.

2. *Cause and effect:* Which comes first in the actualization of self-consciousness—the subject which does the knowing or the objectified "subject" which is known? The question is, of course, a chicken-or-the-egg type of question; neither is first.

We might say that they are "simultaneous," except that the concept of simultaneity usually has meaning only in the context of linear, objective succession. This being the case, we should not expect that the propositions giving expression to the reflections of self-consciousness should be of the same nature as, for example, the conclusions of Aristotelian syllogisms, in which the premises are construed as causally related, and prior, to the conclusions, and the concluding proposition is a kind of encapsulization of this causal relationship. Rather, we should expect a paradoxical type of proposition in which even distant causes are held together with their effects in a state of dynamic reciprocity, approximating simultaneity.

3. *Movement and stasis:* In self-consciousness there is a constant differentiation of the knower from the known, one might almost say a repulsion (in a nonpejorative sense). This is the "movement" of self-consciousness, which, of course, does not involve the usual first-order transition from one state to another. But the process of self-repulsion here requires the entities or aspects repelled to have a certain stability—one might say the highest degree of stability—in order for this process of repulsion, which is constant in reflective activity, to take place. This fact will no doubt lead self-consciousness to be somewhat serious about keeping all the sacrosanct determinations and distinctions of conventional speech and concepts intact; but we must expect occasional paradoxical departures from the conventional, in which stable determinations are "set in motion," so to speak, by that self-ish aspect of consciousness which does not seem to take seriously the rules proclaimed and promulgated by the other, object-oriented aspect.

4. *Being and negation:* It is interesting to note that in Sartrean existentialism consciousness is characterized as a special type of nothingness (the nothingness of freedom) in contrast to the compactness and closedness of being (that which confronts consciousness as something to be negated and overcome); while in the philosophy of Descartes, conversely, we begin with consciousness as the self-evident existent, the only certain being there is, and use this consciousness as a test and criterion for anything external to consciousness, rejecting as tantamount

to "nothingness" that which does not conform to this criterion or pass this test. But in the act of *self*-consciousness Sartre and Descartes both turn out to be right: for self-consciousness thrives on the constant negation and annihilation of its mere being (if it did anything less, it would run the risk of being determined, unfree), but it also functions as the originating existent passing judgment on the reality of all objects in the world, including itself. Thus when Plato speaks in the *Phaedo* of the unity of life and death, or Hegel in the *Logic* about the unity of being and nothingness, the source of their insights seems to be the merger of such absolutely opposite concepts in self-consciousness.

5. *Immanence and transcendence of the ego:* In self-consciousness the ego must depart from itself in a sense in order to circle back upon itself and "close the circuit" to generate the processes of reflection. But like the man who needs something solid beneath him in order for him to jump, the ego cannot depart from itself in the context of the circuit of self-consciousness unless it already possesses itself and, in fact, is identical with itself (otherwise the act would not be consciousness of *self*). Likewise, self-consciousness can only hold on to itself by constantly "standing back from" itself; otherwise it would be arrested in mere being or immersed in the mere consciousness of objects, so that there would be, in effect, no self worth holding on to. Only something that is completely immanent within itself could possibly transcend it*self;* and only something which can completely distance itself from itself could return to lay hold on, and remain immanent in, itself. This final paradox of self-consciousness may perhaps give some intimation as to the experiential springboard for some of the religious paradoxes in oriental religions, and also occasionally in Christian mysticism, which express dissatisfaction with the idea of a God "out there" beyond the world, and strive to coordinate the immanence and transcendence of God in paradoxical ways.

One who is convinced that ordinary logic is not sufficiently equipped to formalize or organize such specifically *self*-conscious operations of the human psyche might feel himself impelled to develop or promote a "dialectical" logic. If he does so, however, he will do best to maintain a certain modesty about the scope and application of dialectic. For example, he should not rush to speculate that a cause could come after its effect or that time could run backwards in the world as objectivized, since such speculations are only appropriate to a domain such as quantum mechanics, in which (as explained by Heisenberg's Uncertainty Principle) it is explicitly understood that our subjective methods and measuring devices are so intertwined with the objects being studied that there is no clear-cut subject/object distinction. In like manner, he should not necessarily conclude that in the world as objectivized black is changing into white, up into down, light into darkness, being into nothingness, etc., since it is only by dint of a great deal of self-conscious reflection that we begin to recognize opposites as changing into one another (being into nothingness, life into death, service into domination, etc.), and the changes that take place in truly Heraclitean fashion are primarily *second-order* transmutations—changes in our concepts which, in an active self-consciousness, sometimes take place almost "before our eyes."

## Dialectic and Ordinary Logic

To say that self-consciousness itself is the epitome or paradigmatic instance of the self-reference and paradoxy of consciousness is not to offer a *solution* for paradox, however, since paradox is no longer a "problem" where this self-reference and paradoxical opposition is not only accepted and recognized, but designated as a *sine qua non* condition for self-consciousness in the first place. The essential "problem" *here* is a second-order problem: the problem$_2$ of coordinating the nonparadoxical logic and language that result from object-oriented consciousness, with the paradoxical thought processes that result from the reflective activities of self-consciousness. This problem, strictly speaking, emerges not from the side of dialectical logic, which is constitutionally equipped for union with its opposite, but from the side of ordinary, nonparadoxical logic, which is not positively equipped for union with its opposite,[3] although its very tendency to determine and limit, if applied to *itself*, e.g., in the extension of mathematical logic to the expression of Gödel's theorem, amounts to a kind of negative preparation paving the way for such a union. But ordinary logic and the science that is its corollary have had a pivotal importance in the development of Western culture and must not be simply abandoned. And since we must all use, and to a great extent subscribe to, this ordinary logic if we wish to avoid a state of mere passive mysticism, the problem turns out to be a real, important, and ineluctable problem$_2$.

The question of the projected complementarity of traditional logic and dialectical logic is quite speculative, since at present there is no standard, universally recognized, and highly developed dialectical logic. Hegel's logic is perhaps the closest approximation to such a goal; but attempts at developing and even formalizing dialectical logic have also been made by Stéphane Lupasco, Michael Kosok, Yvon Gauthier, and others;[4] and if formalization be considered proper to a dialectical logic (a point we must consider later in this chapter), these more recent attempts might be considered preferable to Hegel's.

Even if there were some standard and recognized dialectical logic, it is clear that ordinary logic and dialectical logic could not be "consistent" in the usual (ordinary logical) sense. It is perhaps this consideration that has led Melhuish to warn against compromising dialectical logic at this particular stage of its development. Melhuish points to the Hegelian "syntheses" as an outstanding example of compromise—an Aristotelian compromise insofar as "in contrast to the dynamic contradiction of Heraclitus, Hegel finds it necessary to maintain that contradiction is not a final category and that transcendence of the contradiction is legitimate and necessary."[5] Toms points to two other defects in Hegel's system: (1) the idea of a necessary succession (e.g., in Hegel's philosophy of history), which is based on the fallacious reasoning that if $p$ and $q$ are thought to be contemporaneous, and if $p = \sim q$, the relation of $p$ and $\sim q$ is therefore automatically concluded to be one of succession; and (2) the further unwarranted assumption that this necessary succession is also a *logical* succession just because it is necessitated.[6]

Toms's criticisms may be valid, but Melhuish's criticism of Hegel seems to misconstrue the Hegelian "syntheses" as similar in nature to the syntheses of ordinary logic, which involve compromises resulting from discovering some "lowest common denominator." This is certainly not the case with Hegel's syntheses, which do not do away with oppositions through compromise but preserve and transcend them (through the principle of *Aufhebung*) often in explicitly paradoxical form. The reference of Melhuish to Heraclitus is significant. Although he speaks in places of the complementarity of the two logics, Melhuish is most concerned with establishing a new logic in which, in Heraclitean fashion, indeterminacy rather than determinacy becomes paramount[7] and logical discourse becomes applicable to a "nonselective," uncircumscribed universe containing an actual infinity of things and ideas.[8] In his extreme emphasis on indeterminacy and nonselectivity, Melhuish fails to heed the counsel offered by Leslie Armour, a more moderate proponent of dialectic:

> As one attempts to put together a dialectical system, one must sift and sort ideas on some principle or other. . . . Some ideas will be rejected precisely on the ground that they do not lead anywhere. More importantly, if there are ideas which lack the required links and which lie within the appropriate domain, they will fail to appear in any scheme of this kind just because no ideas lead to them. Hence a dialectical logic might disguise just the viable ideas which opponents of the whole scheme might be supposed to rely on.[9]

Hegel, in contrast, insisted on the absolute necessity of retaining the "distinctions of the understanding" (produced by the straightforward application of ordinary logic), and opted for a "speculative logic" as a synthesis of abstract logic (ordinary formal logic) and dialectical logic.[10] In general, he looked with disfavor on those who thought they had found some way to bypass ordinary logic. This disfavor is exemplified in the Preface to his *Phenomenology* and the last chapter of that work, on "Absolute Knowledge," in which Hegel criticizes Schelling and the intuitionists and the romanticists in general, who want to bypass some or all of the unromantic work of logical argument and logical distinctions.

## Systematization of Dialectical Logic?

The above-mentioned attempts at formalizing dialectical logic are, of course, aimed at giving dialectical logic the sort of definiteness and concreteness that might prepare the way for the coordination and cooperation of the two logics. But serious objections, especially by Hegelians, have been raised because "formalization" seems to be a result of a distinction between subject and object, form and content, that is the keynote of traditional logic, but is not an essential distinguishing feature of dialectical logic. Hegel himself emphasizes that his dialectics should not be considered a "method" applied to some content; and his insistence that dialectical progressions are not just movements of the mind, imposed as a "method" upon external content, but progressions of the mind's subject-matter as well, makes it quite probable that he would not be in favor of any formalization of dialectic. Certainly a proponent of dialectical logic should never hope to devise a proof system in which one could, so to say, produce the exact dialectical opposite of $x$, or to generate an exact paradoxical unity-in-distinction of $x$ and

$\sim x$ by following standard axioms and rules of inference. On the other hand, if there is any validity at all to dialectical logic, some sort (not necessarily the Hegelian sort) of *systematization* of it may be possible; and perhaps that is where proponents of dialectical logic should concentrate their efforts. But we are considering here only the inner necessity of dialectical-paradoxical thinking, abstracting for the present from the possibility of systematization, which will be examined in detail in chapter 4.

# 3

## Paradox and the Congruent Philosophical Expression of Dialectic

The philosophical proposition, since it *is* a proposition, leads one to believe that the usual subject-predicate relation obtains, as well as the usual attitude towards knowing. But the philosophical content destroys this attitude and this opinion. . . . Only a philosophical exposition that rigidly excludes the usual way of relating the parts of a proposition could achieve the goal of plasticity. . . . The sublation of the form of the proposition must not happen only in an *immediate* manner, through the mere content of the proposition. On the contrary, this opposite movement must find explicit expression. The return of the Notion into itself must be *set forth*. . . . The *proposition* should express *what* the True is; but essentially the True is Subject. As such it is merely the dialectical movement, the course that generates itself, going forth from, and returning to, itself.
                    —Hegel, *The Phenomenology of Spirit,* Preface

## Dialectical Logic and Paradox

Whatever may be the proper form for a systematization of dialectical logic, it seems that paradox should have a certain centrality in that logic, perhaps analogous to the centrality of the monadic assertorial propositions in ordinary logic.[1] For it is by means of paradox that we go *beyond* the vague idea of a "unity of opposites" (which emerged among some of the German idealists and the Right Hegelians and some English Hegelians and is still a characteristic tenet in modern idealism)—as Hegel also went beyond that idea—to the kind of unity-in-distinction that seems to be called for by the exigencies of self-conscious reflection, as expounded above. For example, in Hegel's *Phenomenology* the opposition of the realistic approach and the idealistic approach to spatial and temporal presence in the chapter on "Sense-Certainty" is not simply synthesized in the subsequent chapter on "Perception," but is encapsulated in the unity-in-distinction of a paradox in the chapter on "Sense-Certainty," namely, the paradox that the essential reciprocity between the ego and the spatiotemporal world *is* what we call sense-certainty; and the opposition of Master and Slave in the chapter on the "Independence of Self-Consciousness" is not simply synthesized into the "Stoical Self-Consciousness" in the following chapter, but is transcended within the context of the Master-Slave dialectic itself, at that moment when there is a reciprocal recognition on the part of both Master and Slave of the paradoxical facts that the Master's dependence on the Slave is a form of slavery, and that the Slave's dominance over the objective world through his work makes him a free and independent self-consciousness, a Master.

Logicians might claim that such paradoxes are the result of flouting the rules of logic by using terms equivocally. For example, they might challenge Hegel's paradox of sense-certainty on grounds that sense-certainty becomes fluid and oscillating only because it is "put in motion" by the *a priori* sophistry of Hegel's dialectical sorcery; and they might argue that the Master becomes a Slave only if one accepts, like Hegel, the premise that the "freedom" which characterizes the Master is a special very abstract relation of consciousness to objects in the world. But the very inability of the more impeccably logical philosophers themselves to come up with precise and univocal meanings of "sense certainty," "freedom," etc., may be taken as an argument negatively supporting the use of paradox to capture and pinpoint some of the multiple and often opposite meanings or implications of such terms.

## The Varieties of Paradox

True philosophical paradoxes such as the examples from Hegel given above must be distinguished from logical, semantical, and/or grammatically generated paradoxes. The latter express primarily their own inability-to-express (a paradoxical situation that, of course, at the level of pure logic is not considered funny or even paradoxical). The former, however, can express ideas and insights that are meaningful and do not just involve the mind in endless sophomoric gymnastics. The latter result from the conventional and constitutional limits of words and the various connections of words allowed by the laws of grammar, usage, or logic. The former, in contrast, result from the peculiar nature of our concepts, which do not have neat boundary lines separating them in our mind but intermingle unashamedly with their opposites, and even require their opposites for definition and existence.

This intermingling and mutual metamorphizing of opposites noticeable in philosophical paradox is also the distinguishing mark of religious and literary paradoxes. As Rosalie Colie puts it, paradox in all these forms

> exists to reject such divisions as those between "thought" and "language," between "thought" and "feeling," . . . In paradox, form and content, subject and object are collapsed into one, in an ultimate insistence upon the unity of being. . . . One is forced to fuse categories, since paradox manifestly manages at once to be creative and critical, at once its own subject and its own object, turning endlessly in upon itself.[2]

One of the most forceful religious champions of paradox has been Kierkegaard, who contends that paradox is not only essential to the Christian religion but is the definition of Christianity.[3] In the literary domain, some of the New Critics maintained that paradox is essential to poetry. In philosophy, paradox seems to be inseparably connected with philosophy's traditional function of criticizing established meanings and values.

The *explicit* use of paradox, however, is only intermittent in the history of philosophy: for example, by Socrates, who claims to know only the limitations of his own knowledge; by Plato, who argues that we can only know what we already know, that it is better to suffer injustice than to perpetuate it, that the only person who can be safely entrusted with political power is one who does not desire it, etc.; by Heraclitus, who stubbornly maintains not only that one cannot find stability in nature but also that one cannot arrest his movement long enough to say or conceptualize "stability"; and in particular by Nicholas of Cusa and Giordano Bruno, who brought the endemic Renaissance interest in paradox to a head with a metaphysical use of paradox which was both explicit and self-conscious. Hegel, to whom one could point as the major constructor of paradoxes in the history of philosophy, paradoxically enough does not seem to be conscious of any central importance of paradox in his system or in philosophy, but merely seems to have the paradoxes thrust upon him in the process of developing the dialectic (a fact which may arouse our suspicions as to a possible unplanned but inevitable connection between dialectic and paradox). One could give many examples of this in Hegel, but the Preface of the *Phenomenology* will serve as an illustration.

Hegel says there that substance-as-subject is "simple negativity, and thus a splitting up of the simple" (Hoffmeister, ed., 20), and is also a doubling which is "non-diverse and even the opposite of ordinary diversification" (ibid.); that the form of a being like God is "as essential as the essence of that being" (ibid.); that the Absolute is "essentially a Result" [rather than an origin] (ibid., 21); that the "I" is unmediated mediation (ibid.); that purposefulness is "the unmoved, which moves itself" (ibid., 22), and "its beginning is the end, its actuality is its idea or concept'' (ibid.); that the proper refutation of a thesis can come only from its full development, and the proper positive exposition of a principle involves taking a negative attitude to the principle (ibid., 23); that anything is ''unfamiliar, just insofar as it is familiar'' (ibid., 28); that the concrete becomes self-moving only by sundering itself and making itself non-actual (ibid., 29); that Spirit is essentially the process of becoming an other to itself (ibid., 32); that insofar as the existence of a being is a self-identity, it is a self-differentiation (ibid., 8); that science is ''pure self-likeness in self-differentiation'' (ibid.), concrete existence is its logical existence, and the true form is the development of its content (ibid., 10); and that what is negated in a determinate fashion has (and is) a positive content (ibid., 12).

Sometimes even authors who use paradox explicitly in their writings do not seem to realize the full extent of paradoxes they are getting involved in. For example, as Colie points out,[4] Plato's *Parmenides,* which is a paradigmatic example of paradoxical antirationalism, is entirely rationalistic in its thrust.

But *most often* the challenges of philosophy to standard meanings and values have *not* been explicitly formulated *as* paradoxes, although they could be. For example, Descartes' idea that objectivity is grounded in subjectivity became more fully expressed in Kant's deduction of the categories of reality on the basis of logical operations, and then became hypostasized in the maddening Schellingian form of $(+A=B, A=B+)/A=A$,[5] without any of the principals in this evolution being aware that they were dealing with something very paradoxical; and Hume's idea that the ''ought'' must be rooted in some ''is'' has only gradually and intermittently led to efforts to represent the opposites, ''ought'' and ''is,'' as paradoxically implicating each other, instead of mere attempts to reduce one to the other.

Although, as noted above, there seem to be some major ''family resemblances'' among philosophical, religious, and literary paradoxes, there are also some important differences among these varieties of paradox that should be recognized, namely:

1. Philosophical paradoxes differ from religious paradoxes in that they do not depend on any belief-system or mystical experience or state of enlightenment. For example, such sayings in the Gospel as "the first shall be last" and "he who loses his life shall save it" can make sense only if one accepts the belief-system of the Gospel, including the doctrine of an afterlife and the redemptive effects of humiliation, suffering, and death; and Meister Eckhart's references to man's transformation into God could make sense only to one who had the sort of experiences a mystic like Eckhart seems to have had. In the oriental religions, the situation is similar: one must subscribe to a particular religious intuition about the place of man in the world in order to catch the meaning of paradoxes such as "The Spirit is within all, and also outside," or "form is matter" (the *Upanishads*); or "when freed from abiding (with thoughts), you are said to be abiding with the non-abiding" (the *Prajnaparamita Sutras*); or especially the striking and variegated paradoxes of the *Tao te Ching*, such as "Those who know do not talk and talkers do not know," "Choosing hardship, the Wise Man never meets with hardship all his life," or "The Wise Man, having given all he had, is then very rich indeed."

2. Although literary paradoxes, like philosophical paradoxes, are dialectical and challenge received opinions or value systems,[6] they differ in an important way from philosophical paradoxes insofar as they depend on insight and intuition rather than argument. Oxymorons such as "loving hate," "darkness visible," "traitorous trueness," "loud silence," "lonely crowd," or "living death," in the very brevity which is essential to their formulation, seem to preclude any argument whatsoever. Presumably literary paradoxes *could* be argued for; but they would lose their aesthetic appeal and literary value if this happened. This is especially evident in poetry. Argument would trivialize and even destroy paradoxical lines such as

> Careless she is with artful care,
> Affecting to seem unaffected.
>
> William Congreve, *Amoret*

or,

>for I
>Except you enthrall me, never shall be free,
>Nor ever chast, except you ravish me.
>>John Donne, *Lecture upon a Shadow*

and,

>He who bends to himself a Joy
>Doth the winged life destroy;
>But he who kisses the Joy as it flies
>Lives in Eternity's sunrise.
>>William Blake, *Gnomic Verses,* xvii, 1

or,

>So shalt thou feed on Death, that feeds on men,
>And, Death once dead, there's no more dying then.
>>Shakespeare, *Sonnets,* 146

or the following verse from T. S. Eliot:

>Midwinter spring is its own season
>Sempiternal though sodden towards sundown,
>Suspended in time, between pole and tropic.
>When the short day is brightest, with frost and fire,
>The brief sun flames the ice, on pond and ditches,
>In windless cold that is the heart's heat,
>Reflecting in a watery mirror
>A glare that is blindness in the early afternoon.
>And glow more intense than blaze of branch, or
>    brazier,
>Stirs the dumb spirit: no wind, but pentecostal fire
>In the dark time of the year. . . .
>>From "Little Gidding," *Four Quartets*

Colie points to Shakespeare's *King Lear* as an extraordinary clustering of all the standard Renaissance paradoxes.[7] But although it is undeniable that Shakespeare portrays or illustrates a whole host of paradoxes in this play, one could not say that he proves or demonstrates them.[8]

Thus if indeed philosophical paradox is conceptual, discursive, and based on demonstration, it is to be differentiated not only from logical-syntactical, semantical, and/or grammatical paradoxes but also from religious and literary paradoxes.

We must also be careful, finally, to distinguish philosophical paradox from that form of irony in which (a) some situation contrary or contradictory to expectations or intentions emerges; and (b) a dual audience is presupposed, consisting of (i) the initiated, the perceptive, who appreciate what is actually happening, and (ii) the unknowing, the uninitiated who are overtaken by unexpected circumstances. Numerous dialectical developments in Hegel's philosophy are of this nature: for example, when the final key to understanding man's inner nature through "observation" turns out to be the human cranium[9]— an outcome which is expected by the phenomenological observer, but not by the psychologizing consciousness being analyzed; or when the revolutionary consciousness finds it must resort to tyranny to implement its goals;[10] or when the final decision-making power of a constitutional monarch turns out to be the power of dotting the $i$'s and crossing the $t$'s.[11] Compare such developments to the outcome of the Master-Slave dialectic, in which there is not just an ironical metamorphosis of Master into Slave and vice versa, but a reciprocal and simultaneous recognition by both Master and Slave that to be a Master is to be a Slave, and vice versa; or to the final outcome of the *Phenomenology* as a whole, where it is demonstrated that Speculative Science as the ultimate unifier can transcend the essential differentiations of the phenomenological level only if it returns continually to reimmerse itself in those differentiations.

## Philosophical Paradox

Granted that philosophical paradox is to be differentiated from irony and various other categories of paradox, what are the positive, specific, intrinsic features of philosophical paradox? The following four seem to be central:

1. *Syzygy:* Carl Jung used this astronomical term in his psychological theories to characterize the *Conjunctio oppositorum* taking place in the personality as various opposites, such as masculinity and femininity, entered into a dynamic unity-in-distinction. We may perhaps purloin the same term as an appropriate descriptor of the philosophical paradox. In statements such as "Ask yourself whether you are happy and you cease to be so" (J. S. Mill), "the supreme triumph of reason is to cast doubt upon its own validity" (Unamuno), "consciousness is that which it is not, and is not that which it is" (Sartre), "what seems nothing to the intellect is the incomprehensible Maximum" (Nicholas of Cusa), or "the reality is the appearance" (Hegel)—there is a simultaneous conjunction of ideas which would not be permitted to cohabitate if the rules of ordinary logic and usage were being followed.

2. *Nonvicious circularity:* Vicious circularity is a characteristic (and maddening) feature of the liar paradox, the Barber paradox, and other logical or semantic paradoxes. The circularity of philosophical paradoxes, on the other hand, rather than causing frustration and obfuscation, can have the effect of clarification and, in some cases, almost the type of satisfaction that results from problem-solving. For one who follows the arguments in Hegel's *Logic,* the notion that Being because of its absolute *in*determination is identifiable with Nothingness, and that the two terms are constantly metamorphosing into each other, can help to clarify the traditional idea of being-in-general, which is so difficult to grasp conceptually; and Hegel's arguments to the effect that essence and existence are as inseparable and mutually implicating as the circuit of positive and negative polarity in electricity helps to offset the habits of abstraction which lead us to treat of concepts like essence as if they could actually exist in isolation.[12]

3. *Dynamic transcendence:* In paradox we get beyond the mere static opposition of life and death-in-the-form-of-a-corpse, the mind and the-brain-as-physical-object, a culture and its-art-as-mere-external-product—to use a few Hegelian exam-

ples.[13] The emphasis in paradox is on a constructive, dynamic correlativity reminiscent of the paradigmatic interrelationship within self-consciousness of the "I" and the "me." The mind which grasps, on the paradoxical level, the union of being and nothingness, essence and existence, appearance and reality, ignorance and knowledge, domination and servitude, duty and happiness, etc., is set-in-motion, so to speak, to reproduce intellectually the actual reciprocity that obtains between various opposites, as soon as we release them from that more isolated segregated state that is (paradoxically) a prerequisite for its own transcendence.

4. *Demonstrability:* A paradox is not philosophical if it relies merely on religious belief or aesthetic intuitions for its acceptability. If a paradox is philosophical, it must be demonstrable: For example, Kierkegaard's thesis (similar in tenor to J. S. Mill's cited above) that concentration on happiness brings unhappiness is demonstrated at length, albeit informally and indirectly, in *Either/Or*[14]; and the first half of Hegel's *Phenomenology* may be taken as a sustained argument for the anti-Kantian paradox that consciousness, far from being opposite to a thing-in-itself, *is* the unique knowing and knowable thing-in-itself.

## *Philosophical Paradox and Dialectical Logic*

Finally, it would seem that while many philosophical paradoxes are a predictable result of a dialectical logic, there are a certain few paradoxes which are pivotal or central, insofar as they sum up or epitomize the basic insights of dialectical logic, in much the same way that, for example, NC and EM are intuitions that sum up the insights that gave rise to ordinary logic in the first place. The following paradoxes would seem to be central in this sense:

1. *There can be no similarity without difference,* and maximal similarity is unthinkable without maximal difference: One

can perhaps think of two objects in the inorganic world, e.g., two stones indistinguishable in shape and distinguishable only in position and minor discrepancies in their constituents, as the extreme of minimal differentiation, concomitant to some basic and obvious similarities. But one can also discern an extreme of minimal similarity, a similarity (between two beings) that is rather unimportant and uninteresting, although easy to comprehend, e.g., the similarity of a star with a bird, in the context of some overarching, obvious differences. The more complex and interesting similarities illustrate what Teilhard de Chardin calls the "law of life," namely, that "unity differentiates," i.e., that the most consummate examples of unity are organisms and consciousnesses and thinking processes, in which greater unity goes hand in hand with greater complexification and differentiation. An ineluctable element of differentiation is to be found even in the tautologies of ordinary logic, as thinkers as diverse as Hegel and Wittgenstein have brought out;[15] and it is incontestable that the differences among the ideas coordinated and identified in our ordinary language are even greater than the elementary tautological theorems of logic. But the propositions of ordinary logic and the statements of ordinary prose are not remarkable for bringing out in an explicit way the differences, oppositions, even contradictions which they entail. Paradoxical statements or propositions, on the other hand, do accomplish this; this is their peculiar and unique contribution to thought. In philosophy, the process of demonstrating these paradoxes in some systematic way by exploring the boundaries, so to speak, of language, logic, and concepts leads to a paradoxical or dialectical logic. This latter logic does not circumvent or supersede ordinary logic but, on the contrary, depends on the validity of ordinary logic, the *boundaries* and *limitations* of which function as the precise area of its concentration, or the indispensable starting point for its investigations.

2. *There can be no difference without similarity:* This is the counterpart and corollary of the observations in the preceding paragraph. Obviously, if two things were so different that they were worlds apart, there would be no basis for comparison, and

they could not even be designated "different." Maximal differences are only able to emerge where the basis for comparison is evident and solid; and this implies a substantial bedrock of similarity. This is why a paradoxical or dialectical logic, which is orientated to bringing out differences in a maximal way, is correspondingly maximally dependent on ordinary logic, to which is entrusted the task of preserving the self-identities, the uniformities of words and ideas as much as is possible, in the face of a world without and within, which is undergoing constant changes.

3. *The primordial and paradigmatic opposition is the unity of subject and object:* The unity of subject and object, in which we are all caught up, is also so evidently a state of opposition that it functions as the primal intuition upon which the validity of any paradoxical or dialectical logic is based. The category of S/O unity is susceptible to its initial and primordial differentiation on the basis of three possibilities regarding the emphasis on S and O, respectively. These three possibilities can be represented graphically as O = S, S = O, and (O = S) = (S = O):

a. O = S: This is the schema or formula that summarizes the paradoxical notion that being is thought—the notion that in Western philosophy was originally and enigmatically formulated by Parmenides, who tells us that it is the same thing to be and to be thought. Perhaps the most illustrative contemporary application of Parmenides' basic insight is to be found in Heisenberg's Uncertainty Principle, which gives evidence that the entities or states of affairs we examine are to a great extent dependent upon the theories, procedures, and instruments we employ in the examination of them. This principle, as was mentioned in chapter 1, has been applied primarily to microcosmic phenomena, but it is not limited to such phenomena.

b. S = O: This formula encapsulates the revolutionary insight of Descartes, that thinking is existence. Perhaps the paradigmatic contemporary application of this insight is to be found in psychoanalytic theories, which portray the conscious and free decisions and acts of human beings as manifestations of latent or repressed residues existing in some individual or collective "unconscious."

c. $(O = S) = (S = O)$: This shorthand expression, which is a kind of dialectical synthesis of (a) and (b) above, has both a first-order and a second-order significance: As a first-order synthesis, it is typified most concretely by language, in which subject and object meet in a special and unique way, and in which all the problems attendant upon this meeting seem to converge. For language is a paradoxical unity of external and internal, sound or symbol and conceptual meaning; the cause of paradoxes (grammatical, logico-syntactical, semantical, and/or epistemological); the solution to paradoxes (because it can be used as an instrument to designate and pinpoint the identities and the differences that make paradox what it is); and the greatest obstacle to the solution both of verbal or logical paradoxes and of philosophical paradoxes (because of entrenched conventions, and the fact that language, science, and the function of analysis, as opposed to synthesis, have been accidentally intertwined).

In its second-order significance, finally, the above formula gives us an interesting example of the way that dialectical synthesis differs from the sort of synthetic combination that might emerge on the level of ordinary logic. For if we take into account the translations of $S = O$ and $O = S$ that were given above, we might take the third and longer formula, $(O = S) = (S = O)$, to refer simply to some synthesis of organisms and consciousness, or perhaps of evolution and unconscious drives. But this would not be a dialectical synthesis, because it would not transcend its own initial levels of oppositions. Rather, the formula takes us into a different level entirely (i.e., the level of language), which does not appear arbitrarily (it does presuppose both the organic sphere and the sphere of consciousness, but does more than just fuse the opposites that it presupposed). For language alters the nature of the opposition and both defuses and intensifies the opposition which it "synthesizes."

There is some *prima facie* similarity between the central propositions just discussed and the tautological propositions which function as theorems in ordinary logic and are used to generate other propositions in accord with the laws of inference. However, one could not strictly characterize the central paradoxes of dialectical logic as "theorems" or "axioms," because this implies the before-and-after, antecedent-consequent, foundation-and-superstructure motif of ordinary logic. It would be more congruent to say that they are pivotal but nonfoundational paradoxes that both initiate, and will continue to be produced by, any paradoxical logic.

# 4

# The Systematization of Dialectic

> If it can be claimed for a philosophical system that it is
> "successful," what this means is that some universal
> need of philosophy, which could not engender philoso-
> phy on its own, wended its way by a kind of instinctive
> propensity to the aforementioned system. If, on the other
> hand, the need in question had been able to bring forth
> philosophy on its own, it would have already been *satis-*
> *fied*—by creating its own system.
>
> —Hegel, *The Difference Between Fichte's and*
> *Schelling's System of Philosophy*

> Unless it is a system, a philosophy is not a scientific
> production. Unsystematic philosophizing can only be
> expected to give expression to personal peculiarities of
> mind, and has no principle for the regulation of its con-
> tents. Apart from their interdependence and organic
> union, the truths of philosophy are valueless, and must
> then be treated as baseless hypotheses, or personal con-
> victions. Yet many philosophical treatises confine them-
> selves to such an exposition of the opinions and senti-
> ments of the author.
>
> —Hegel, *Minor Logic,* §14

Before turning in the next chapter to a consideration of Hegel's
dialectical system, we will consider the exigencies of a philo-

sophical "system" in general—including also dialectical systems, but as a separate category. For if dialectic and its often paradoxical conclusions have a validity of their own, the possible systematic interconnection of this method and its conclusions or results may differ in important respects from the sorts of interconnections to be found in nondialectical systems.

## An Initial Dilemma for the Systematizer

The development of a system, as Hegel himself notes,[1] seems to be a natural outcome of the synthesizing propensities of the human intellect, carried to their logical conclusion. The intellect, experiencing its own powers of synthesis, may suppose that it is somehow within human grasp to develop a complete and consistent system encompassing everything important that can be said about the world. But as Hegel notes, like Gödel a century later, an initial hard choice between completeness and consistency confronts the potential synthesizer at an early stage:

> At first, empirical science envisages scientific totality as a totality of the multiplex or as completeness; while a strict formalism envisages it as consistency. The former can at will elevate its experiences to universality, and can push the consistency of its putative determinations up to the point where other empirical matter (which contradicts the first but has just as much right to be excogitated and expressed as a principle) no longer leaves room for the consistency of the preceding, and compels its abandonment. Formalism can extend its consistency so far as is generally made possible by the emptiness of its principle, or by a content which it has smuggled in; but thereby it is in turn entitled to exclude what lacks completeness from its apriorism and its science, and proudly revile it as "the empirical." For

formalism asserts its formal principles as the *a priori* and absolute, and thus asserts that what it cannot master by these is non-absolute and accidental.[2]

And so we have, when it comes to the implementation of synthesis, a natural dichotomy between the "empiricists," who pursue completeness without trying to systemize their findings in a tightly self-consistent manner, and the formalists, who concentrate on developing an impressive self-consistent network from a few abstract, *a priori* principles, and point to everything outside their neat systematizations as "unessential," "merely empirical." Thus it is no wonder that, in our time as also in Hegel's, there has been a reaction against the more ambitious synthesizers, the "generalists," who tend either to emphasize formal consistency at the expense of empirical completeness, or to bring in all manner of empirical data so loosely related that it is impossible to "see the forest for the trees."

The awareness, implicit or explicit, that one would almost certainly have to acquiesce in gross incompleteness in order to erect a formally consistent general system, seems to have led to specialization as a reaction. For example, in both the "hard" and "soft" sciences, it is a matter of considerable pride to be recognized as a specialist in a certain area or subarea, and occasional generalists such as Teilhard de Chardin in paleontology and Arnold Toynbee in history are ignored or lambasted by their more specialized colleagues, in spite of (or possibly even because of) widespread popular approval. In contemporary Western culture, specialization proceeds apace, only occasionally challenged by the work of generalists like Fritzof Capra in physics, John Kenneth Galbraith in economics, and Douglas Hoffstadter in computer science.

But the specialists themselves do not completely eschew synthesis. Rather, one could say that one of the best reasons for specialization is to make possible a complete and self-consistent synthesis *in a certain well-defined area*. The more the area is narrowed down, the better the chance there seems to be to attain both completeness *and* consistency within it. The electrical engineer, the molecular biologist, etc., precisely by focusing on well-defined and highly specialized areas, are able to keep all the data in their area optimally manageable and all the theories of their discipline consistent in their interconnections.

Thus the specialist, by a kind of strategic humility, has produced the most successful and widely accepted syntheses, by reacting against synthesis in the larger sense, the synthesizing operations of the generalist. But there still seems to be a need for the latter, i.e., for the generalist who can not only satisfy the human desire to see the general framework and context for the various types of progress being made in the world of knowledge, but also help the specialists to make connections among themselves, possibly to avoid overlapping and reduplication of efforts, possibly even to derive inspiration through cross-fertilization of ideas or a new ecumenical sense of collegiality. But can the generalist attain what seems to be impossible—a combination of completeness with methodical self-consistency?

## Modern Attempts at Synthesis

Before even beginning to discuss various synthesizing attempts in the modern world, we encounter an initial problematic presupposition: Synthesis is taken to be the antipode to analysis. In common parlance "synthesis" has become synonymous with the operations of collecting and unifying, including the mental operations concerned with collating and interrelating ideas; "analysis," conversely, is taking things apart, mentally and even physically, isolating component elements for purposes of inspection, categorization, etc. In logic and philosophy, concerned with the basis for making judgments, the distinctions between synthesis and analysis which were made by Immanuel Kant in the eighteenth century, and are still largely accepted, are most relevant: synthesis is the type of unity created in our ideas when they are expanded to encompass new data from new experiences,[3] while analysis is the isolation of concepts from experience, examining them for pure conceptual content and conformity to the law of non-self-contradiction.[4] In chapter 5 Hegel's extension of this basic Kantian division to the idea of a "synthetic" and "analytic" method will be discussed. But it should be noted for the present that both the philosophical and the more general usages of "analysis" and "synthesis" presuppose a hard and fast distinction between the two operations. This distinction, as we shall see, is questioned by some, and may have to be jettisoned in the case of some putative dialectical systematization.

Most contemporary attempts at synthesis seem to be "synthetic" not always in the strict Kantian sense, but in the first, most general sense, i.e., insofar as they are attempts to bring about unity and organization in knowledge, in order to offset the excessive splintering, professional myopia, and noncommunication existing *among* the various specializations in the sciences, mathematics, philology, etc. (although each individual specialization, *considered in itself,* might be the epitome of unity and organization). This tendency is exemplified currently by the search for a unified field theory to give greater coherence to various branches of physics and cosmology; by the still new science of ecology to coordinate the physical, life, and social sciences; by the search for viable economic, political, and social approaches to world organization by world-order theorists; and perhaps most notably by general systems theory (GST). The latter, originally developed by Ludwig von Bertalanffy as a nonmechanistic and nonvitalistic approach in biology,[5] has been applied with varying degrees of success to the social sciences, engineering, cybernetics (with which it is sometimes too easily identified), and other fields. Those who are engaged in such synthesizing activities might be called "generalists" insofar as they are mainly concerned with the more general coordination among and interactions between disparate specializations, disciplines, or subsystems. But they

are also in a sense specialists insofar as—analogously to the
physician who completes extra training leading to board cer-
tification as a "general practitioner"—they "specialize" in the
function of analyzing certain specific areas for the purpose of
*general* interdisciplinary coordination and verification of data
and procedures. Quite clearly, it is in such pursuits that the
usually dependable distinctions between generalist and specialist, synthesis and analysis, begin to dissolve.

## Systematization in Philosophy

In view of some of the successes of GST in biology, engineering, international relations, and other fields, it would not be
unreasonable to pose the question, "Why not a 'systems-
philosophy'?" The major proponent of the application of GST
to philosophy at present is Erwin Laszlo, who argues that, in
reaction to excessive and one-sided analysis in philosophy, "a
return must be effected to synthesis: not as a vast mastery of
specialized knowledge, but as a systematic philosophical assimilation of information of extra-philosophical origin. Philosophical synthesis can mean the conjoining of various sets of
nonphilosophically researched data, to furnish new avenues
toward the constructive discussion of substantial philosophical
issues."[6] In particular, Laszlo criticizes the tendency of philosophers to operate in a vacuum, ignoring the relevant data and
methods of the sciences, and undertakes a demonstration of the
way that scientific findings concerning the integration, self-
stabilization, self-organization, and hierarchization of natural
systems can be profitably utilized to throw light on traditional
philosophical problems such as the mind-body relationship, the
fact-value distinction, the purpose of individual and social
human existence, etc. He is optimistic about the ability of
individual "generalists" to bring about very comprehensive
scientific-philosophical syntheses; but, like Hegel and Gödel,

he also recognizes the thorny dilemma of the synthesizer in coordinating completeness and consistency:

> Theories which combine empirical ideals of accuracy with the rational ideals of economy, consistency and generality have the edge over theories that sacrifice one component for the sake of others. Those that sacrifice the rational factors become *ad hoc* and their scientific status is correspondingly lower. . . . Others, which sacrifice empirical accuracy for the rational component's elegance and heuristic, strain credulity and belong to the realm of rationalist theology and metaphysics. Somewhere between these extremes lies the ideal of a scientific theory, where empirical and rational ideas are optimally combined. Systems philosophy belongs to this range.[7]

Laszlo does seem to achieve a convincing combination of the empirical with the structural in his synthetic endeavors; but, using Laszlo's own principle of "economy," the traditional philosopher might protest that these results should be characterized as "metascience," with some admixture of metaphilosophy, rather than as "systems philosophy."

It has to be admitted, however, that most traditional philosophers have not been any more successful than Laszlo in bringing about the well-nigh-impossible combination of empirical richness and formal organization. Most of the traditional philosophers noted for "system building"—one thinks of Spinoza, Fichte, the late scholastics—have gone to the extreme of emphasizing formal consistency, often at the expense of empirical attunement.

Laszlo points to the philosophies of Plato, Aristotle, the scholastics, Whitehead, and Bergson as milestones in the evolution of "a systematic and constructive inquiry into natural phenomena on the assumption of general order in nature."[8] One might agree with this assessment if it were granted that the scholastics in question were the early scholastics, concerned with developing a synthesis relying on the then-prevalent Aristotelian natural science; and if it were also agreed that some of the philosophers mentioned went *far beyond* the objective of making "an inquiry into natural phenomena." But the inclusion of Plato in the list also poses a *prima facie* problem: Would there not be a significant difference in the construction of a system by a synthesizer like Bergson, and by a more committed dialectician like Plato? Would not an explicitly dialectical system, if such an entity be conceivable, differ in important respects from a "linear" or nondialectical system?

## Dialectical Philosophy and Systematization

As we saw in chapter 2,[9] Melhuish takes exception to the Hegelian "syntheses," and considers them to be nonfatal but serious compromises of the Hegelian "nonselective," dialectical methodology. Melhuish opts for a pure dialectical, "Heraclitean" approach, explicating and/or generating antitheses and oppositions, without the arbitrary and compromising imposition of a synthesis. If we follow his reasoning to its logical conclusion, we would have to say that a "dialectical system," if it involves a massive *synthesis* of oppositions, is self-contradictory—a self-nullifying extension of dialectic.

Melhuish would be right in his criticism of Hegel, if a Hegelian "synthesis" connoted a simple unification or integration of opposites. But Hegel himself considers such a concept of synthesis "unscientific."[10] Indeed, as was argued in chapters 2 and 3, the Hegelian syntheses are unities-*in*-opposition; and more often than not what is generated are paradoxes, in which the oppositions are not just abolished but preserved and transformed.[11]

In any case, since a dialectical methodology has (by definition, it would seem) the capacity to combine with *its* own opposite, it should be easier for such a methodology without compromise also to incorporate straight logical synthesis than for ordinary formal logic to incorporate dialectic.[12] And, so unlike Melhuish, we need not necessarily envision a separation of nonselective, indeterminate dialectical philosophizing from philosophizing in the more usual sense, and from the ordinary logic on which it depends. One who engages in the elaboration of dialectic must do so, as Leslie Armour counsels,[13] without prejudice or presuppositions.

But the question still remains: What form or forms can or should an unprejudiced systematization or elaboration of dialectic take? If we were to broaden our search to include *unsystematic* (albeit ingenious) attempts at dialectic, we would no doubt want to include the ancient polemical paradoxes of Zeno, the rhetorical dialectic of the sophists, the paradoxical insights of Heraclitus, and, in modern philosophy, the aphorisms of Nietzsche. But if we confine ourselves to a search for the *clearly* systematic attempts, the following forms would be important milestones in the development of dialectical systematization:

1. *Socratic dialogue:* This may be considered the originary dialectic, the matrix from which Western philosophy has been derived, only to become oblivious, all too soon, of its origins in living conversation in ordinary language. In the opinion of Hegel,[14] it is also a very capricious form of dialectic, relying, as it does, on the immediate, living contact of individuals exchanging ideas in a contingent, *ad hoc* manner, and unable to withdraw to the "pure regions of thought" to develop all the necessary dialectical connections. (If Hegel is right, we might conjecture that the Socratic dialogue is the closest approximation to that pure, "nonsynthetic" dialectic advocated by Melhuish.) Socratic dialogue was "dialectical" in the most technical sense through its use of *elenchus*—the methodical interrogatory testing of one's interlocutor for contradictory presuppositions, with a view to leading him through awareness of contradictions to the truth. But it was also dialectical in a more basic, albeit implicit, way, simply by bringing into proximity

different individuals with differing opinions, working toward
some kind of *rapprochement*. Richard Rorty, recognizing the
importance of such ordinary dialectical encounter for philosophy, would like to raise it to the status of a paradigm. Rorty
characterizes philosophy itself as essentially "conversation"
writ large. According to Rorty, philosophy is just

> a "voice in the conversation of mankind," . . . which
> centers on one topic rather than another at some given
> time not by dialectical necessity but as a result of various
> things happening elsewhere in the conversation (the
> New Science, the French Revolution, the modern
> novel) or of individual men of genius who think of
> something new (Hegel, Marx, Frege, Freud, Wittgen-
> stein, Heidegger), or perhaps of the resultant of several
> such forces.[15]

A final stage in the development of philosophy-as-conversa-
tion, according to Rorty, is the quasi-institutionalization of
"edifying philosophy"—the sort of philosophy exemplified in
the work of Kierkegaard, William James, Dewey, the later
Wittgenstein, and the later Heidegger.[16] These philosophers are
contrasted most sharply with more traditionally "systematic"
philosophers, such as Descartes, Kant, Husserl, and Russell,
who argue for a "point of view" and work to produce some
final, definitive interpretation of reality. The edifying philosophers, in contrast, avoid definitive statements or formulas, and
strive rather through "reactive" means, including satires, par-
odies, and aphorisms, merely to "keep the conversation
going." Through their "systematic" renunciation of system-
building, Rorty maintains, they have paved the way for the
revitalization of the philosophical enterprise in the contemporary world.

"Deconstruction," as practiced and expounded by Jacques
Derrida, is explicitly contrasted with (and employed upon) the
Hegelian sort of dialectic which (claims Derrida) is oriented
toward "closure" or absolutely comprehensive syntheses. But

in a very real sense deconstruction, like the hermeneutics of
Hans Georg Gadamer, is an extension of philosophy as "conversation," specifically as applied to the systematic cross-
examination of the thoughts of *others,* and as such is reminiscent of the originary Socratic dialectic, in which the philosopher
as "midwife" inserts himself into the contingencies and uncer-
tainties of the conversation of others, to shake up established
opinions, and possibly to help bring forth ideas which will be
adjudged viable or alien by the communal consensus.

Derrida, however, is a more radical "gadfly" than Gadamer
and other hermeneuticists, who do not give up completely on
the possibility of definitive interpretations. Derrida, in his de-
constructive reading of texts and comparison with other texts
(including the "intertexts" of, e.g., socioeconomic facts), and
in his advocacy and utilization of "dissemination" (textual
criticism comparable to Freud's investigation of the "dream-
work" of the unconscious), churns up traces of strange philological "displacements." Derrida also replaces the traditional
'representation' of epistemology with 'différance', a neologism
indicating the disparity and delay between sign and signified.[17]

Derrida's deconstruction includes criticism of the systematic
totalities of "logocentric metaphysics,"[18] but is not properly
antisystematic or fragmentary, since "différance" and other
"undecidables," being outside the traditional dichotomy of
"system vs. antisystem," constitute a totally other "system of
ciphers that is not dominated by truth value."[19] Rodolphe
Gasché observes that Derrida's "infrastructures" (i.e., undecidables) "form chains; they can and must be systematized
up to a certain point. . . ." Moreover, "since it [the space of
infrastructures] lies beyond the opposition of system and fragment, whole and part, infinity and the finite, it also constitutes
the systematicity of systems."[20]

Derrida in his concentration on infrastructures is not primarily concerned with the "dialectical" oppositions and contradictions that occur in the (supra)structures of discourse, but
such oppositions and contradictions do occur (even occasionally in Derrida's own texts). One might say that they are an

epiphenomenon or presence in both Socratic dialectic and dialectic as "conversation." Analysis of the actual (supra)-structures of discourse has been the concern of structuralists like Foucault and Sève. Michael McCanles, drawing on the work of structuralists as well as deconstructionists, develops a "dialectical" model of discourse to demonstrate how both contrariety (which entails an opposite) and covert or implicit contradiction (that which authors would like to exclude) are generated in texts. According to McCanles, the very endeavor to create well-formed (noncontradictory) texts leads to terms and statements which instigate not only contrary assertions but also the specific contradictory assertions they are meant to exclude; so that the more narrowly and precisely the texts are formed, the more expanded their "countertexts" become. McCanles shows how the use of such a dialectic model of transformation can "staticize," for the purposes of analysis, the inherent dynamics of contradiction in language.[21]

It should be noted that the latter "dialectical model," as well as Derrida's "deconstruction" and Rorty's more generalized "conversation" all differ from the original implicit "Socratic" dialectic in one important respect: they eschew, or at least are not overtly concerned with, the presentation of "truth," which is made synonymous with a "point of view." It is a fact that some commentators have also characterized Socrates himself as avoiding the presentation of truth. But Gregory Vlastos has argued convincingly that Socrates himself, while avoiding the championing of a "point of view," nevertheless at least implicitly aims at truth by the systematic elimination of everything but the true premises which each individual already *has* concerning moral matters—an epistemological position that Plato finally brings out explicitly on Socrates' behalf in the *Gorgias*.[22] "Truth" in this sense is something that resides in actual human beings, but needs to be brought out by dialogue. Gadamer's hermeneutic "truth," in somewhat similar fashion, resides in the texts of tradition, but needs to be brought out by the community of interpreters.

2. *Platonic dialectic:* In Plato's dialogic accounts of the life and

conversations of Socrates, we must first distinguish an explicit dialectic from an implicit dialectic. The explicit dialectic, heartily advocated and propounded by Plato himself, is the dynamic relationship of finite, fallible men with transcendental truth and goodness, to be attained in a maximal way only by the strenuous, highly disciplined intellectual-spiritual odyssey of "dialectic," the process by which one forges above illusion and illusory opinions to true principles or ideas.[23] But the implicit dialectic in Plato has to do with the primary *means* by which one rises above opinion to truth on the "upward path" of dialectic; namely, through the highly structured but not readily apparent constructive engagement taking place constantly (just as it took place between Socrates and his interlocutors) between Plato and Socrates, and, in a more indirect fashion, between Plato and Homer, Protagoras, Parmenides, and other major luminaries whose ideas were still having an influence in Plato's day.

The charisma of Socrates was so great that it would have been unthinkable for Plato to write a dialogue in which he himself was one of the interlocutors, on an equal footing with Socrates; and so unfortunately we do not have any unmistakable indication in regard to most issues as to where Socrates leaves off and Plato begins. But it is still important to recognize that Plato is not to Socrates as Boswell was to Dr. Johnson. With Plato we move from a Socratic dialectic, which is essentially "soft" insofar as Socrates refrained, at least overtly and for the most part, from advancing any position of his own, to a "hard" dialectic, which involved a systematic "testing" of Plato's own points of view against the views of contemporaries and predecessors, as well as against the tentative views of Socrates, i.e., the views that Socrates as "midwife" allowed to surface among his interlocutors. Plato on the one hand wanted to avoid "forcing" Socrates' views or truths into a preconceived mold, but on the other was not willing to be a self-effacing "midwife" for Socrates' ideas. The result was a dialectical relationship even more intense than that between Socrates and his interlocutors.

It is this second form of dialectic, only implicit in the work of Plato, which is most important from the point of view of dialectical systematization. It is also a form of systematization intermittently practiced among contemporary professional philosophers when they go beyond analysis and criticism, to a true constructive engagement in depth, with the luminaries relevant to their own milieu. Examples might be the dialectical *Auseinandersetzung* of Heidegger with Plato and Kant, of Gadamer with Aristotle, of Sartre with Flaubert and Saint Genet, of Derrida with Rousseau and Hegel. One element unfortunately lacking in most of these post-Platonic dialectical-literary engagements, however, is the explicit use of the dialogue form, which is now almost the exclusive province of dramatists. Part of the power of Plato's dialectical thinking may be due to his effective use of dialogue; certainly the explicitly dialectical format contributed by dialogue, especially a dialogue in which oneself, or some effective and credible adversary, is included as a participant, may be an effective vehicle for the continuation of this particular form of dialectic, as I have argued elsewhere.[24] The use of an explicit dialogic format for the presentation of dialectic would seem to be not only appropriate but advisable if, as J. Hintikka maintains, the dialogue is both the historical source and the paradigmatic model for all major forms of dialectic.[25]

3. *Aristotelian dialectic:* "Dialectic" for Aristotle is a continuation of the "upward path" of the explicit dialectic in Plato, but as a systematic endeavor connotes primarily a conscientious and methodical sifting of common or influential opinions pro and con on a given controversial topic. If one compares this concept of dialectical methodology with the "implicit" dialectic of Plato, discussed above, he can see a continuity between the two conceptions. To a certain extent the Aristotelian conception explicates the dialectical presupposition, already implicit in Plato: that we must confront, for the purposes of assimilation, refutation, or reinterpretation, the thinkers who constitute the mental horizons of our culture. This idea becomes explicit in Aristotle's *Topics* and other logical works. With Aristotle, dialectical confrontation becomes more systematic

and extensive, while losing something of the depth and intensity it had in Plato. Aristotle is not as continually and intensely engaged with Plato or any other individual thinker as Plato was with Socrates. Rather, with Aristotle the dialectical process becomes a methodical analysis not only of the opinions of Plato but also of Thales, Anaximander, Parmenides, Heraclitus, and many others—as a means-to-an-end, a necessary propaedeutic for arriving at truly scientific conclusions. Thus in the *Physics, Metaphysics, Nicomachean Ethics,* and other works of Aristotle, the initial chapters are characteristically given over to an analysis of the chief opinions relevant to the issues being discussed.[26] Only after a thorough examination of these opinions, and some attempts to find some sort of an acceptable reformulation of the problems and a formulation of his own preliminary position regarding the problems, does Aristotle forge ahead to a gradually more "scientific" treatment of his subject (comparable to the "path downward" from the Ideas in Plato's explicit dialectic).

This dialectical-propaedeutic methodology of Aristotle reached its most highly organized, systematic form at the hands of Thomas Aquinas and other early and middle scholastics. In the *Summa theologiae* and other works of Aquinas, Aquinas develops his own position only after systematically enumerating and discussing the chief actual, relevant positions in opposition to his own. Scholasticism and Thomism in modern times abandoned in spirit this initial dialectical stage, giving attention only to the opposed positions in *Aquinas's* milieu or the milieu of later scholasticism, ignoring or giving a succinct dogmatic "refutation" of opposed modern positions. Mortimer Adler and his colleagues, in their twentieth-century efforts to revitalize Thomism, have brought about an amalgamation of the Aristotelian idea of dialectic[27] (without the systematic Thomistic enumeration of *Videtur quods*) with some of the more fundamental or "perennial" Thomistic positions. In order to fully restore the Aristotelian-Thomistic approach in contemporary philosophy, however, one would need to engage in a more presuppositionless analysis of positions pro and con, in which

Aristotelian or Thomistic positions were given no automatic privileged status. It would seem that some modern counterpart of the highly structured Thomistic literary form, ritualizing engagement with contrary positions, would be conducive to, and perhaps even necessary for, the optimal systematization of this form of dialectic. This is especially true if, as McLuhan theorized,[28] a connected lineal sequence such as ordinary printed prose tends to inculcate, whether we intend it or not, the correspondingly lineal thought patterns associated with formal (nondialectical) logic.

4. *The systematization of paradox:* All three of the forms of systematization just considered have to do in some way with making an appropriate response to diversities of interpretation and the possibility of utilizing, organizing, or controlling this diversity. The result should be optimally some particularly viable, if not impregnable, vision of reality which would go beyond the mere clashing of the positions, to an explication of their antitheses, if not an actual synthesis. It has been suggested above (see page 36) that the paradoxical proposition, because of its close connection with dialectical processes, may be a particularly apt instrument, if not a necessity, for capping off dialectical oppositions. One might even suppose that by beginning with a *paradoxical thesis* already incorporating major oppositions or conflicts in its formulation, one could hope to present a kind of conceptual summation of the major intellectual conflicts going on, and perhaps ensure a certain impregnability to one's own more nuanced presentation. A step in the direction of this approach to systematization was made by Martin Luther in arguing for his ninety-five theses, at least some of which lived up to Melanchthon's description of them as "paradoxes."[29] Further steps were taken by Nicholas of Cusa (Cusanus) and Giordano Bruno, who were strongly affected by the widespread and almost endemic interest in paradox in Renaissance cultural circles. The "coincidence of opposites" propounded by Cusanus and Bruno (sometimes in the form of literary dialogues) took on a variety of forms and applications—the unity

of finite and infinite, knowledge and ignorance, identity and difference, sense perception and soul, actuality and possibility, maximum and minimum, subject and object, even physical qualities like hot and cold. Such *coincidentia* may have been too often oversimplified and misunderstood by interpreters, especially in the case of Cusanus, as Jasper Hopkins argues in a recent book.[30] And their dialectical objectives are often subordinated to larger objectives in cosmological, metaphysical, or ethical theorizing. But the not-infrequent subsystems in their works concerned with the scientific demonstration of paradoxical formulations uniting, or tending to unite, concepts which in Aristotelian dialectic would have been referred to different schools of thought or perspectives serve as an important bridge to the highly systematic, conceptually-oriented and -generated dialectic of German idealism at the outset of the nineteenth century.

5. *Hegelian dialectic:* In Hegel's writings there are elements of both the implicit Platonic and the explicit Aristotelian dialectics referred to above. For example, Hegel's *Faith and Knowledge* and *Difference between Fichte's and Schelling's System of Philosophy* are *Auseinandersetzungen* with Jacobi, Fichte, and Schelling after pattern #2 described above; Hegel's *Phenomenology of Spirit* is both a methodological and a vigorously sustained sifting of opposed positions regarding the nature of certainty and truth, with a view to arriving at a scientific presentation of "Absolute Knowledge"—a didactical process which can be understood as an extraordinarily personal, possibly idiosyncratic[31] exemplification of pattern #3. But the dialectic of Hegel's mature system is best understood as a sophisticated and highly systematized further (and perhaps ultimate) extension of pattern #4.

The unique interpretation of dialectic characteristic of Hegel received its remote historical inspiration from the doctrine of Heraclitus, who came closest among the ancients to understanding the intrinsic, conceptual unity of opposites,[32] but the more immediate historical underpinnings for the dialectic of Hegel (and also of Fichte and Schelling) is to be found in the Kantian doctrine of the "antinomies," as Hegel himself indicates.[33] In his analysis of the "Antinomies of Pure Reason,"[34] Kant argues that the differing of opinions or positions, which is the hallmark of the versions of dialectic discussed above, is simply a symptom of an underlying characteristic of thought itself: the abstract propositions of the understanding, when all their implications are brought out by reason, naturally and inevitably, as Hegel puts it, "veer around into their opposite."[35] Thus dialectical opposition is not due primarily to the antithetical perspectives or subjective dispositions or stubbornness of thinkers, but to the thoughts they are thinking, which are *intrinsically* dialectical. In order to systematize *this* form of dialectic, something more than dialogic interaction or the sifting of opinions is necessary. One might conceivably start with the most abstract idea and show, or rather allow the idea itself to show, how it veers paradoxically into its own opposite, and ultimately coordinates opposition, as more and more concrete stages of the idea are reached. This is the self-imposed task of Hegel's dialectical system of philosophy, which will be considered in detail in the next chapter.

6. *Marxism and the Systematization of Dialectic:* In the preceding analysis of systematization in dialectical philosophy, a certain evolution or continuity of development may be discerned from (1) dialogue and conversation, geared implicitly or explicitly to disclosing oppositions or contradictions, with or without specified methods for resolving conflicts; (2) intense intellectual engagement between two thinkers, with or without the use of literary dialogue; (3) sifting of the opposed or disparate opinions of others by a single thinker as a prelude to a "scientific" presentation of his own theses; (4) incorporation of a variety of usually opposed ideas into paradoxical formulas, loosely or tightly interconnected; and (5) concentration on the dialectical unity-in-distinction of conceptual oppositions, deductively organized in their interrelationships.

Marxism, however, which at least *prima facie* seems to represent one of the most ambitious modern attempts at the systematization of dialectic, also seems to involve an abrupt departure from the aforementioned continuity of development in the concept of dialectic in Western philosophy. For it is not concerned with opposed opinions or viewpoints or ideas but with "contradictions" in material reality and/or with "dialectical" methodologies oriented to controlling, promoting, or solving these contradictions on a practical or theoretical level. There is also in Marxism an overt opposition to philosophy per se, as an ideological offshoot of "alienation," so that the categorization of Marxism as a *philosophical* systematization of dialectic is problematic from the outset. But at least from the Western "bourgeois" philosophical standpoint, Marxism and its philosophical antecedents (especially the eighteenth-century Enlightenment and nineteenth-century idealism) are inseparably intertwined, and Marxist claims should at least be considered in any analysis of the possibilities of dialectical systematization.

Marx spelled out his own interpretation of his relationship to Hegelian dialectic fairly clearly in his *Grundrisse* (notes from 1857–58) and his *Zur Kritik der politische Ökonomie* (published in 1859). Among other things he states his resolve to use what Hegel called the "synthetic" method—proceeding dialectically from the abstract to the more concrete—without succumbing to any of the Hegelian "illusions" about reality being constituted by the ideal. Marx utilized this methodology in *Capital*, volume I (1867), even over the objections of Engels, who was afraid critics, unaware of the nature of dialectical progression, would take the early stages of the dialectic developed in volume I as a final statement. (Since volumes II and III were published posthumously, Engels's apprehensions turned out to be well grounded.)

Marx's employment of dialectic, which he refers to as the "method of science,"[36] is evident in *Capital* in his frequent reference to "contradictions," "antitheses," and "oppositions" in the capitalist system which supply the springboard for further conceptual development. The general conformity of Marx's *Capital* to the categories and development of Hegel's Logic was evident to Lenin and Stalin and has been commented on by some modern interpreters.[37] Friedrich Engels, who extended the Marxist approach into a dialectical-materialist philosophy of nature, portrayed Marx himself as a social scientist using a post-Darwinian natural-science approach and applying "dialectics" to the relevant data from political economics.[38] If we keep in mind that the German term *Wissenschaft* then (and even, to a certain extent, now) did not imply any sharp separation between philosophy and empirical sciences, that Marx had a strong admiration for Darwin's theory of evolution (although not for extrapolation of "survival of the fittest" and "struggle-for-survival" explanations to social phenomena), and that the Hegelian dialectical system which Marx purported to utilize after it had been properly rescued from its "upside-down" presentation of reality incorporated much data from the empirical sciences, and was characterized by Hegel himself not only as "science" but as the archetypal Science—Engels's portrayal of Marx is worth considering.

However, simple acceptance of Engels's view is no simple matter, since debates about the continuity between Marxism and Engelian doctrines and about Engels's interpretation of Marx's intent and objectives have been continual. While Thomas Sowell considers Engels a "faithful interpreter" of Marx's thought[39] and Sean Sayers defends Engels from allegations of a mechanistic and reductionistic interpretation of Marxism,[40] Norman Levine, while acknowledging that most American scholarship is "unanimist" (emphasizing a continuity between Engels's and Marx's views), himself feels it necessary to join the "divergent camp,"[41] and European "revisionist" Marxists very often take pains to emphasize the alleged distinction of the "dialectical materialism" of Engels from the "historical materialism" of Marx himself (Marx never used either of these terms to describe his vantage point).

With the not infrequent rejection of Engels's Marxism and/or of his rather complex interpretation of Marx as a post-Darwinian dialectician in the sphere of socioeconomic evolution, multiple disputes have emerged as to what dialectic—let alone dialectical systematization—signifies in Marx, and even as to whether dialectic has any import for Marxism at all. While, for example, Norman Levine looks upon dialectic as *the* most important aspect of Marx's thought,[42] and Scott Meikle defends the possibility of a "dialectical materialism"[43] while Richard Norman allows for a dialectic in nature of identity and difference, quantity and quality, etc.,[44] on the other side Lukács, Ruben, and Schmidt maintain that "dialectic" in nature is confined to the Subject-Object relationship,[45] Vásquez focuses on an intrinsic, conceptual dialectic in *Capital* which goes beyond historical dialectic,[46] and Colletti and Schmidt deny the possibility of a *materialistic* dialectic entirely.[47] Daniel Little claims that Marx does not follow the dialectical method at all, even in *Capital,* where he seems to employ it explicitly,[48] and Richard Hudelson joins Vlope, Cohen, McMurtry, and many others who believe Marx's *Capital* can best be understood as *ordinary* science, "dialectics" being limited largely to Marx's intermittent summarizing of some results of research, most of his analysis *not* being developed according to any specifically dialectical methodology.[49]

Jacques Guillaumaud, echoing Louis Althusser's insistence that dialectic is just a remnant of idealism and has not facilitated one discovery in the natural or human sciences, poses a question extremely relevant for Marxists today:

> The "dialectical laws"—are they or are they not laws of nature? If the answer is "yes," how do we explain their scientific sterility? . . . If the answer . . . is "no," this answer entails on the one hand an explicit disagreement with an Engels and a Lenin . . . and, on the other hand, an eradication of dialectic.[50]

Thus, even to many Marxists, it is not completely clear that Marx's *Capital* is indeed an example of the systematization of dialectic; or, if it is, whether the methodology applies to the work as a whole, or merely to intermittent summaries; and, if it does apply to the work as a whole, whether it also applies to Engels's extensions of Marxian dialectic, with Marx's knowledge and apparent approval, to the realm of nature.

Robert Solomon in his *The Spirit of Hegel* maintains that Hegel—in spite of his conscious motivation and declared intentions—was a crypto-atheist. One might perhaps maintain similarly that Marx—in spite of his apparently sincere protestations to the contrary—was an ordinary, nondialectical social scientist, a crypto-scientist. Until depth psychology gives us clear access to the prevarications of the unconscious, however, it would no doubt be most prudent to grant to Hegel that he was a good Lutheran and to Marx that he *was,* in fact, engaged in *some* form of systematic and dialectical analysis of social and economic antitheses in capitalism, and of the emergence of new socialistic relations which would resolve the major conflicts and reverse the primary alienations.

Notwithstanding, there are still some final questions about whether a dialectical "methodology" can really be successfully extracted from Hegelian logic and applied fruitfully to mundane phenomena, in the way that Marx and Marxists *purport* to do. In this regard, Klaus Hartmann observes:

> Hegel's philosophy attains its evidential culmination just insofar as it is maintained in the medium of the Logos, or more precisely in the medium of Categories; and just insofar as it demonstrates a logical self-organization of the categories. . . . [With Marx] "the actual" means the "total actuality" from the standpoint of realism, not the mere categorial actuality, i.e. being elevated into the Concept. [The claim that] "the actual is the rational" is no longer understood [by Marx] categorially, but in the fashion of realism.[51]

To be sure, Hegel himself speaks of "contradictions" or "antinomies" (meaning more precisely contraries or contrariety[52]) in objects,[53] in chemical interactions,[54] in cosmology,[55] in the ethical and legal sphere,[56] etc. But as William Maker emphasizes, even in Hegel's philosophy of nature, which is the externalization of the "Idea," nothing extrinsic to the Idea of nature is introduced, and we are in fact not dealing at all with external things or individuals.[57] Maker objects:

> It is in fact Marx, and not Hegel, who propounds a mystified idealism. . . . [Marxism] takes what is properly understood as a feature of the relation of categories or determinacies in systematic philosophy . . . and reads it into reality and history as an allegedly empirically discoverable feature of them. . . . This amounts [to] imposing the rulership of ideas or philosophy over reality.[58]

Maker's critique thus ends up converging with the opposition of certain Marxists, some of whom were referred to above, to dialectics within Marxism. If Hegel himself had used categories like "the transformation of quantitative progressions into qualitative changes," or "the interpenetration of opposites" as hypotheses to be applied methodically to the analysis of external reality, this methodical procedure could conceivably be taken over successfully and used to analyze or generate transformations in reality. But for Hegel even "reality" is a category of systematic philosophy, systematically analyzed; the Hegelian "method" is the method emerging uniquely from the categorical content rather than applied to it; and the "objects" treated are to be received only from within the system, not from outside. Hegel's dialectic is not taking place in the external world.[59] There may be oppositions and even contradictions which must work themselves out in the external world, but the dialectic that Hegel is interested in presenting in his system is something taking place only in the world of the spirit[60] (although it cannot be denied that, since Spirit is in the world, the dialectic of Spirit can have unpredictable, contingent mundane effects).

Marx's use of dialectic was complex and nuanced, and not

subject to simple classification. Certainly he was not a dialectical philosopher or a historian or a social scientist or an evolutionist or social evolutionist in any of the usual senses; nor could it be said with any precision that *Capital* and other later works were history, or natural history or political economics. But in another sense all these characterizations are applicable, and Engels's view, which skirts conventional classifications to highlight Marx's unique personal synthesis, may be not inappropriate after all.

In spite of the above-mentioned doubts raised by critics as to Marx's seriousness about dialectic, it is quite certain that he employed dialectic, relied on it to give force to his arguments, and in fact attempted to systematize its use in *Capital*. However, Marx's use of dialectic was rather eclectic, and his attempts at systematization were relativized by this eclecticism. The "eclecticism" becomes manifest when we consider that (1) Marx's scheme (discussed in his *Grundrisse* and various letters) for proceeding from the abstract to the concrete in six stages is modeled after the latter sections of Hegel's *Philosophy of Right;*[61] (2) the Marxian "dialectical progression" from feudalism to capitalism to socialism is based on the Hegelian idea of dialectical progression in history (e.g., from the Roman "spirit" to the Germanic "spirit") or in the sociopolitical sphere (e.g., from bourgeois society to the state bureaucracy); (3) Marx's antithetical presentation of the capitalist-worker relationship is a very extensive variation on the "Master-Slave dialectic" in Hegel's *Phenomenology;* (4) Marx's use of categories like the dialectical emergence of qualitative change from quantitative changes to explain, e.g., the way that the extension of the maximum number of hired hands in the workplace led from feudalism to capitalism is taken over from Hegel's *Logic*, along with what might best be described as "moments" or "occasional features" of Hegel's *Logic*, such as "the negation of the negation", the "interpenetration of opposites" (applied by Marx to, e.g., use value and exchange value in commodities), and the intermittent intensification of oppositions to the point at which they became self-destructive rather than complementary; (5) Marx applies Hegel's occasional "dialectical inversions" to, e.g., the phenomenon whereby the invention and acquisition of labor-saving machinery leads not to the shortening of the working day but to its lengthening; and (6) Marx discerns a multiplicity of "dialectical contradictions," e.g., between money as circulating medium and as individual incarnation of social labor, or between capital as product of, and also as independent from, the circulation of money—which are reminiscent of the frequent "contradictions" or "antithetical moments" generated in Hegel's *Encyclopedia* and *Phenomenology*. (Some strange omissions from Marx's dialectical apparatus are the dialectics of private property and communism, capital and state power, and revolution and totalitarianism, to be found in Hegel's *Phenomenology,* §§430–31, 494–97, 587–92.) Marx's strategic eclecticism with regard to dialectic seemed to work, however.[62] Subsequent Soviet and Maoist "diamat" theorists, trying to produce a more rigidly precise and scientific system of "dialectics", have had to compromise or sacrifice the flexibility, and openness to factual input, that characterize Marx's own eclectic approach.

When a Hegelian considers the gigantic empirical-dialectical systematization essayed by Marx, he is apt to recall the Gospel admonition, "don't put new wine in old wine skins," "don't sew new patches on old material." Marx's empirical data burst the bonds of their Hegelian trappings. If there are indeed important and essential contradictions or antithetical tendencies in the body politic, or even in nature itself, is it possible that we might produce a nondogmatic, empirically oriented systematization of such dialectical "givens"? Among Marxist biologists Levins and Lewontin have come closest to this goal in their *The Dialectical Biologist.*[63] With profuse examples not only from biology but from other physical sciences and the socioeconomic sphere, they strive to illustrate omnipresent dialectical relationships between part and whole, subject and object, equilibrium and instability, internal and external, individual and social, organism and environment, and also show applications of overall dialectical laws of historicity, interpenetration of opposites, universal interconnections, and elemental heterogeneity. However, we find no notable systematicity or organization interconnecting their own multifarious dialectical insights. In Gödelian and Hegelian terms, they seem to proffer a completeness of dialectical information at the expense of strong, consistent conceptual organization.

There is also the additional problem that, with information about "dialectics" of a factual nature in the world of experience, we seem to have gotten far away—perhaps too far—from the traditional and still-conventional meaning of "dialectic." For "dialectic" has traditionally applied to thought or aspects of thought. Is it not an overextension of "dialectic" to apply it to the physical and social world, just as it would be stretching the limits of logic to speak of "logical" processes in nature or "logical conclusions" in social developments? In any case, Hegel, as if in anticipation of the difficulty or impossibility of producing a satisfactory dialectical system of first-order phenomena, sharply restricted his system to the Categorial or Conceptual level, producing an apparently broad but really quite restricted internally organized dialectical network of concepts in which the collation and elucidation of strictly factual data would have to remain peripheral.

# 5

# Hegel's Dialectical-Paradoxical System

The method of truth which comprehends the object is indeed quite analytic, since it remains strictly with the Concept; but it is just as surely synthetic, since, through the [dialectical-speculative] concept, the object becomes determined dialectically, as "other". . . . The foundation [for further dialectical development] is . . . simultaneously a result. . . . The beginning, since it itself is a determinacy over against the determinacy of the result, should be taken not as something immediate, but as mediated and derived; this [process of mediation] can appear as the demand for an infinite *backwards* progress in proof and inference; . . . a result [also] emerges from this new beginning, so that the advance rolls on *forwards* into infinity. . . . The mediating process returns *through* a *content* as if through an apparent *"other"* to itself, to its beginning; . . . the result is the superseded determination, and therefore also the restoration of the original indetermination. . . . The Concept . . . *preserves* itself in being other, the universal *maintains* itself in its own particularization (in the process of judgement, and in reality). . . . Each new level of *self-relinquishment*, i.e. of more extensive *determination*, is also a self-return, and the greatest extension is simultaneously a higher intension. . . . That which leads itself into the simplest profundity is the mightiest and most comprehensive. The highest most concentrated apex is *pure personality*,

which . . . makes itself into the simplicity which is the
immediacy and universality from which it began.
—Hegel, *The Science of Logic,* II.3.3

If the above protracted, multifaceted concatenation of Hegel's
descriptions of his own system seems overwhelmingly complex, the appearance of complexity is due to a string of paradoxes which can be isolated, highlighted, and listed as follows:
Hegel's analytic method is simultaneously synthetic; the foundation of his system is also its result; the beginning, which
should be (by definition) unmediated, is mediated; the indeterminacy of this beginning is, as it were, a determinacy over
against that which results from it; the infinite backwards movement involved in the process of mediation is also an infinite
forwards movement; the goal of the mediating process is to
return to its beginning; the determinations produced through
mediation bring about a restoration of the original indetermination; the Concept, in becoming other to itself, preserves itself;
the universal, in becoming particularized, remains universal;
self-relinquishment is self-return; extension is intension; the
greatest simplicity is the greatest comprehensiveness; and the
highest apex of the entire system of Science is pure personality,
which reestablishes contact with simple immediacy.

One who has read Hegel's *Phenomenology, Science of
Logic,* and/or *Encyclopedia* will be used to paradox and so will
not be overly surprised by such descriptions *per se.* But here we
find that certain conceptions concerning the *very nature of a
philosophical system itself* are also paradoxical. We see that, if
there is a "dialectic of ideas themselves," and if there is a way
of organizing such ideas in a philosophical system, the master
idea *for* such a system will also apparently be paradoxical in a
paradigmatic sense.

As we saw in chapter 4, systematic dialectic as applied to
ideas themselves, rather than to the relationship among thinkers
with differing opinions, began to gain the ascendancy in the

work of Cusanus, Bruno, Kant, Fichte, Schelling, and Hegel. Out of this group Hegel distinguished himself by being dedicated not only to systematizing this type of dialectic but also to creating a system which would obviate the "completeness/ consistency" dilemma (discussed in chapter 4), as well as other dilemmas and dichotomies, such as the Kantian problem of the "thing-in-itself" and the dichotomy between faith and reason.

The early plans which led to such a system date from Hegel's period of collaboration with Schelling. In a letter from 21 November 1800 he mentions to Schelling that he was being forced out of his youthful preoccupation with the "ideal" and his interest in political issues and was committing himself more to the objective of making philosophy into a "reflective" system.[1] In 1802 Hegel points to a proper and healthy "nihilism" (a constructive, progressive form of skepticism) as the means by which finite and one-sided (largely Fichtean) subjectivism could achieve its self-elevation beyond the impasses in which it found itself.[2] Hegel's first major application of this "self-elevating nihilism" was in his *Phenomenology of Spirit,* which he intended to be the first part of his "system," and which would subsequently be followed up and completed by a logic, philosophy of nature, and philosophy of spirit.[3] Hegel's original conception of the specific role to be played by the *Phenomenology* in his system underwent some vicissitudes. But he never explicitly retracted his initial statements about the role of the *Phenomenology,* and the latter work does seem to be an important and integral part of his total system, as I have argued elsewhere.[4] Thus it would seem offhand that Hegel's total system is essentially quadripartite, with the last three parts (the system proper) eventually taking on the form and the title of an *Encyclopedia of Science* (published in three editions—1817, 1827, and 1830). But this partitioning is arbitrary and tentative. If, as Michael Petry argues,[5] the 1807 *Phenomenology* is an immature, expendable youthful introduction, the *Phenomenology* might not be worthy of inclusion; but if the *Phenomenology* is considered to be important in its own right, its major triadic or dyadic divisions could be included in the reckoning; and if, as

Denise Souche-Dagues maintains,[6] the *Phenomenology* is just one of three systematic totalities (the other two being (1) the Jena *Logic, Philosophy of Nature,* and *Philosophy of Spirit,* and (2) the later *Encyclopedia*), one's divisions and enumerations might reflect this fact. But whatever principles of division and enumeration we adopt, we must first devote some attention to Hegel's conception of what is meant by a ''system,'' and his own self-understanding concerning the difference between his own system and other systems, philosophical and nonphilosophical, before going on to elaborate the unique and paradoxical aspects of the Hegelian system.

## The Various Senses of ''System'' in Hegel

1. *Nonphilosophical systems:* Hegel's discussion of nonphilosophical systems revolves largely around a distinction between ''analytic'' and ''synthetic'' methodology—a distinction which, Hegel will argue,[7] dissolves when a dialectical-speculative philosophical system is perfected.

The Hegelian distinction between the ''analytic'' and ''synthetic'' method[8] bears some resemblance to the Kantian distinction between analytic judgments, which are concerned with purely conceptual distinctions, and synthetic judgments, which have to do with the enlargement of our concepts in and through experience.[9] The Hegelian distinction also resembles, in its larger outlines, Kant's own well-known distinction (clarified in the second edition of his CPR) between analytic method, which begins with a concrete object or experience and works back to its *a priori* conditions, and synthetic method, which follows the converse route from *a priori* to *a posteriori.*[10] But Hegel's definition is a bit broader than Kant's: The analytic method, says Hegel,[11] starts with a concrete object or problem, and analyzes it into the relevant universals, forces, laws, or genera of which it is the concretion. The synthetic method begins with the concrete universal (the genus, the law, etc.) and (1) specifies it precisely through definition, (2) elaborates the natural divisions which distinguish the *definitum* from other things or suppositions, and (3) constructs by demonstration a theorem which brings to a conclusion the synthetic processes and the necessity of connections. Examples of the use of analytic method would be the separation of elements in chemistry or the distinction of problem-solving operations in arithmetic; an example of the use of synthetic method would be the development of the Pythagorean theorem from proofs which involve definition and division. Hegel, like Kant, finds the clearest and most relevant models for the use of analytic and synthetic method in the physical sciences and mathematics.

The development of a *system* in nonphilosophical disciplines is primarily a result of the employment of the synthetic method.[12] By means of system-formation, man is enabled in some limited way to mirror the world, which is itself a massive system in which everything is related to everything else.[13] This objective is easier to accomplish when the theme is abstract and relatively simple—as in geometry, which "has an easy task in giving definitions," and to which alone "belongs in its perfection the synthetic method of finite cognition."[14] (Modern theorem-oriented systems of mathematics and predicate logic would seem to be further examples of what Hegel called a "synthetic" system.) As the subject matter becomes richer and more complex, it is more difficult to apply the synthetic method, and the hard and fast separation of synthesis from analysis is more difficult to maintain; but systematization through synthesis is still possible and even necessary. For example, with reference to the science of law, Hegel observes that the denial of the possibility of systematization

> is not only an insult; it also implies that not a single individual has been endowed with skill enough to bring into a coherent system the endless mass of existing laws. The truth is that it is just systematization, i.e., elevation to the universal, which our time is pressing for without any limit.[15]

This example from the sphere of law is a good illustration of the relative murkiness of the analytic/synthetic distinction when it is applied to the more concrete, complex areas of life. Obviously, the systematization of laws that Hegel opts for would involve a great deal of dependence on the "analytic" method—analysis of existing laws to determine categories, genera, sources, purposes, etc.—at least as a preliminary to the process of forming them into a "single system." A fortiori, such tenuousness of the analytic/synthetic distinction prevails also in *philosophy*, which exceeds even the legal sphere in complexity. In fact, both the analytic and synthetic methods turn out, in Hegel's estimation, to be *completely "unserviceable for philosophic cognition."* [16]

2. *Philosophical Systems:* In spite of the insuperable difficulties involved, certain philosophers *have* attempted to use analytic or synthetic methods in their philosophizing. Christian Wolff made a mockery out of philosophy by his unrestrained determination to apply the synthetic method. The paradigmatic example of a philosopher who used the synthetic method with *some* measure of success is Spinoza, whose use of the procedures of demonstration appropriate to geometry resulted in an impressive pseudosystem, hampered by arbitrary presuppositions, e.g., concerning being (extension) and thought, a rigid formalism ill-suited to philosophical thinking, insufficient conceptual mediation, and failure to follow his own major principle ("every determination is a negation") to its logical conclusion (i.e., to the negation of the negation). Schelling also, like Spinoza, used the synthetic method in a semispeculative manner. [17] An example of a philosopher who applied the analytic method to philosophy would be John Locke, who in his *Essay on Human Understanding* tried to investigate thought in an empirical way in order to isolate and classify its essential or universal elements. [18] Thus we might characterize Spinoza's *Ethics* as a magnificent but futile attempt to attain the consistency of a synthetic system, at the expense of empirical comprehensiveness, and Locke's empiricism as a rich store of analytical investigations, without any clear unifying principle.

Other philosophers, ancient and modern, although fortunately free from irrelevant pressures to adopt an exclusively analytic or exclusively synthetic method, have nevertheless failed for various reasons to produce a philosophical system that would combine comprehensiveness with consistent derivation and organization. For example, Plato's interesting mathematical speculations in the *Timaeus* were not really comprehensive enough to accommodate a philosophy of nature, as they purported to do.[19] Aristotle's teaching concerning the natural and spiritual universe, on the other hand, was an extensive, truly comprehensive "series of particular conceptions, which are external to one another, and in which a unifying principle, led through the particular, is wanting."[20] In modern philosophy, Descartes elaborated principles of mathematical physics which are applicable to some extent to the mechanical realm but by no means to organic entities.[21] In Hegel's own more immediate philosophical milieu, Fichte elaborated some admirable systematic principles for a subjective coordination of subject and object, but he failed to produce the philosophy of nature which alone could furnish the requisite objective coordination.[22] Thus the consistency of Fichte's system was maintained at the expense of completeness. Fichte opted for a tightly articulated conceptual fabric "in which nothing empiric was to be admitted from without."[23] But the very extremity of this "idealism" leads it ironically into a kind of absolute empiricism, insofar as it can achieve a semblance of completeness only through some "extraneous impulse" which will "give filling to the empty 'mine',"  i.e., to the elaborate abstract articulations of the pure Ego.[24] Schelling, on the other hand, placed the emphasis on the content, on truth conceived objectively,[25] while the rational superstructure is merely "presupposed,"[26] as an immediate, unelaborated intuition,[27] applied in a merely external way to give the semblance of rational order to empirical contents.[28] As a consequence of the extremity of his approach, Schelling was forced, like Fichte, to edge ironically into a diametrically opposed position: He had to resort to a bastard idealism, casting the multifarious results of his investigation into an intuitively grasped "absolute indifference of subject and object," in which, as it were, "all cows are black" and all empirical details are forced arbitrarily into unity or consistency.[29] Thus, even in spite of these final magnanimous efforts of Fichte and Schelling, Western philosophy had still failed to produce a system which could claim *both* rigorous and consistent conceptual articulation *and* empirical or objective completeness and comprehensiveness.

The reasons for this failure were, in Hegel's view, partly external and partly internal. Externally, a certain historical evolution of philosophies, each with limited, one-sided principles or insights, is necessary before a refined, no longer one-sided system of philosophy assimilating all the one-sided principles can emerge.[30] Internally, some philosophers simply failed to make use of the resources they had at hand to develop at least a relatively full-fledged system. The most conspicuous example of this latter syndrome is probably Aristotle, who failed to utilize fully his own seminal theory of "self-thinking thought."[31] It would have conceivably been possible for Aristotle to use this conceptual breakthrough as an organizing principle by means of which the interconnections of the universal and the particulars in the world could be elaborated, thus producing a truly consistent and unified *as well as* comprehensive system, relative to the state of culture in his era.[32]

In any case, in the modern (Hegel's) era both the external conditions (the historical progress of the basic insights of philosophy to their most refined development[33]) and the internal conditions (our own awareness of the limitations of the principles on which previous philosophies were based) made a final, genuinely balanced system of philosophy possible; and indeed, as we have seen, approximations had already been made to such a system through Fichte's dialectical-speculative elaboration of Kant's philosophy and Schelling's incomplete revision of the Fichtean philosophy.[34] Hegel's major contribution, then, as he perceived it, was to carry forth the efforts of these immediate predecessors one step further, producing a system of philosophy which would encompass and assimilate previous philosophies,[35] or rather, simply point out and expound *the* system, *the* dialectical organization of philosophy which has been developing all along from the earliest times.[36] The function of the philosopher, according to this interpretation, is not to *create* a system (as Spinoza endeavored to do) but to research and recapture the main articulations of the dialectical dialogue/conversation that has been going on perennially in philosophy. One might argue that the resultant system is "complete" insofar as it arrives at its pivotal concepts and theses through an exhaustive empirical investigation of individual and social consciousness, such as takes place in the *Phenomenology;* and that the system is "consistent" in the sense that, rising above the incessant oscillation taking place between subjective certitude and objective truth, it remains on the level of "Absolute Knowledge" and consistently elaborates the dialectical-speculative Concept associated with this type of knowledge. But it would be more accurate to say that, just as the terminological distinction between "analytic" and "synthetic" is no longer relevant when applied to the sort of philosophical system Hegel has in mind, neither is the distinction between "consistency" and "completeness"—which runs parallel to a form-content distinction—any longer viable. This paradox, and others as well, will become more intelligible as we turn now to an investigation of the key idea, topic, and theme which, on Hegel's account, is to be found continuously, throughout ancient, medieval, and modern philosophy, as a kind of central, architectonic paradox.

## *The Originary Paradox in Hegel's System*

We saw in chapter 2 that the experience of self-consciousness seems to be the paradigmatic paradox, and quite possibly the matrix out of which the sort of paradoxes associated with dialectical thinking are generated.[37] For in a direct and immediate fashion, self-consciousness involves a merger of major opposites—subject and object, cause and effect, identity and difference, etc.

It is the experience of self-consciousness that seems to have given rise to the concept of the ''Subject-Object''—a central idea in the philosophies of both Fichte and Schelling, and the apparent springboard for Hegel's initial prognostications about the possibility of a system. Fichte, striving to carry forth the critical philosophy of Kant in such a way as to avoid the dilemma of a *thing-in-itself* always standing outside cognition, had based his own philosophy on the intuition of a ''Subject-Object,'' the analysis of whose dialectical relationships were supposed to lead in an orderly way to the derivation of an entire system of knowledge.[38] Schelling, perceiving that Fichte's Subject-Object was *subjectively* generated and thus not sufficiently presuppositionless, proposed to counterbalance Fichte's ''subjective'' Subject-Object with an ''objective'' Subject-Object through a philosophy of nature.[39] Hegel sees this as the major insight and contribution of Schelling (although Schelling himself eventually fell short of his objectives for constructing a system[40]), and Hegel *portrays the central concept of his own later ''system'' as but an extension and incorporation of the Subject-Object.*[41]

Hegel himself, however, goes beyond the confines of the Fichtean-Schellingean idea of a Subject-Object to the somewhat more comprehensive notion of the unity-in-distinction of *being and thought*—a notion for which Hegel develops the shorthand technical expressions, ''Concept,'' ''Idea,'' and ''Reason.'' ''Concept'' is perhaps the most intrinsically expressive of these terms, since etymologically in German *Begriff* (from *greifen*) connotes a ''grasp'' or ''grasping-together'' (possibly ''comprehension'' would be the most exact rendering), which Hegel applies specifically to the grasping-together of the opposition between being and thought, and other associated oppositions.[42] This ''concept'' for Hegel is *not,* as in ordinary parlance, a thought separate from reality, but incorporates reality. Hegel employs ''Idea'' as a more advanced development of Concept, and ''Reason'' (*Vernunft*) becomes the special supermediating faculty[43] which self-consciousness possesses for comprehending the synthetic totality of the concept and "objectivity.''[44] Hegel's system of philosophy is concerned only with presenting totality in this latter sense—neither the totality of objective determinations nor the totality of determinate concepts, but the Concept's own unity-in-distinction of concept and objectivity, thought and being, in the totality of its manifestations and interconnections.[45] And it is the special task of modern philosophy to make this unity of thought and being explicit.[46]

As mentioned above, there is in Hegel's view one single dialectical system of philosophy which has been unfolding itself in history from the earliest times. One way of presenting this sort of "system" would be through a didactical presentation of its conceptual development, with minimal emphasis on the historical connections. But one might also present such a system with an emphasis on its historical evolution in and through individual and social *consciousness,* touching on the conceptual articulations of the system as an offshoot of the historical progression itself. It is this latter approach that Hegel had adopted in his *Phenomenology of Spirit.*[47] The ambiguity that later developed as to whether the *Phenomenology* should be considered the "First Part" of, or an "Introduction" to, the "system" (Hegel had originally ambivalently characterized it in both ways), or a middle part of the system (one might draw this conclusion from an inspection of its place in Hegel's later writings) is due in part to the impossibility of clearly separating these two approaches, given Hegel's historical-conceptual notion of a single philosophical system.[48] In any case, the paradoxical unity-in-distinction of thought and being in the Concept, the Idea, and Reason may be seen as the main theme continued and expanded in the development of both the *Phenomenology* and the later systematic works, although there is the following notable difference of approach and emphasis in the former and the latter:

*The thought-being thematic in the phenomenology:* In the Introduction to his *Phenomenology of Spirit,* after criticizing

Kant's undue separation of thought and being which resulted in the artificial problem of the "thing-in-itself," Hegel presents as a philosophical antidote his own starting point—self-consciousness itself, the paradoxical unity-in-distinction of concept and object, consciousness and thinghood, thought and being.[49] Then in the body of the *Phenomenology* he proceeds to show how this paradoxical relationship develops in and through its multiple variations—"ego and object," "subject and substance," etc. In "Sense-Certainty" the awareness of "thisness" is shown to involve an interplay between the ego and the object; in "Lordship and Bondage" individual consciousnesses become related to each other as subject to object; in "Rational Observation" self-consciousness looks to the external world for reflections and confirmations of its own certainty of the identity of being and thought; in the section on rational individualization (chapter V.C) consciousness finds in work a means of creating the unity of thought and being; in "Spirit" human society is presented as an initial synthesis of thought and being which gradually begins to undergo disruptions which require more and more sophisticated devices for recapturing some semblance of that initial synthesis; in "Conscience" a final ethical harmonization between the individual and his milieu is portrayed; in "Religion" the unity of being and thought is shown to evolve through various stages to its culmination in the Christian doctrine of the God-man; and finally, in "Absolute Knowledge" a speculative system is adumbrated which will combine the highest stage of subjectivity (exemplified in the subjective Fichtean synthesis of thought and being) with the highest stage of substantiality (exemplified in the Christian synthesis of humanity and divinity).[50]

*The thought-being thematic in the encyclopedia:* In the system proper—the logic and philosophies of nature and of spirit of the *Encyclopedia*—Hegel begins with the philosopher's concept of *"being,"* that epitome of abstraction which is reached by a thorough *thought*-negation of all particular *beings;* and thus, in a very real sense, is tantamount to nothingness. From this initial paradox Hegel then proceeds, just as he did in the

*Phenomenology,* to derive more and more sophisticated results of the *interaction and conjunction of being and thought* until, at the end of the logic, this interaction and conjunction itself is explicitly recognized and designated by the technical term, the "Idea"; but *this* Idea, since it actually encompasses being, encounters no incongruity in presenting itself objectively as nature; and nature, in its turn, eventually unfolding itself in organisms as living and thinking beings, shows that it itself is a full embodiment of the Idea. Finally, the emergence of anthropic spirits in the organic world receives its fitting dialectical complement from the state as a more complex incarnation of the distillations and traditions of multifarious human spirits; and the gradual objective accretions of culture find their ultimate subjective summations in art, religion, and philosophy, in which being, at the terminus of its long progressions, is fully assimilated by self-conscious thought; and this latter assimilation receives permanent, objective expression in the highest products of human culture.[51]

It has already been noted, with reference to Marxism in chapter 4, that these two progressions of the being-thought complexus in the *Phenomenology* and in the system proper are *not* "first-order" progressions. In contrast to Marx, Hegel does not offer us a systematic treatment of a material dialectic taking place in nature or social evolution or history, in the direct clash of people and events in the world. Thus Hegel cannot be portrayed with any exactitude as a proponent of "evolution," whether physical or social.[52] In the *Phenomenology,* when Hegel proceeds in the chapter on "Observation" from inorganic to organic nature and thence to human physiology and psychology, he is talking not about an evolution in nature (like Darwin) or even about an evolution in our knowledge of nature (like, e.g., Thomas Kuhn in *The Structure of Scientific Revolutions*), but about something much more complex and nuanced—namely, the evolution of Reason in its search for an external reflection in nature of the inner synthesis of being and thought which it has brought about. In the *Philosophy of Nature,* when Hegel treats in great detail a progression in nature from mechanical to physical to organic forms, he is not talking about an evolution which has taken place in the material world, but about the evolution of the Idea of nature from the earliest stages in which the union of thought and being was expressed in an ''abstract'' way through the quantitative and mechanical formation of matter to the more advanced ''concrete'' stages, in which the fact of the union becomes maximally manifested. Thus although Hegel seems to be an arch-generalist touching on every conceivable thing in his system, he is in a more precise sense a specialist who confines himself strictly to an examination of a single third-order phenomenon[53]—the progression of the Idea of the unity-in-distinction of thought and being.

Derrida, in *The Margins of Philosophy,* obliquely poses the question: If Hegel's system is concerned with the transcendence (*relevance, aufheben*) of all limits, what then are the limits of Hegelian philosophy? Derrida himself suggests an answer: The writing-down of Hegel's ideas, e.g., the translation of *aufheben* into the French *relever* (meaning both ''elevate'' and ''substitute''), illustrates a ''différance'' which not even Hegel can transcend.[54] But Hegel does seem to recognize the ''différance'' in the written word (see, e.g., the *Phenomenology,* M§§95, 97, 110), and the unmediatable difference of death (M§188). Hegel himself states: Whatever is outside of, or not relevant to, the speculative Idea (an example of this would be the contingencies of Nature, discussed in the *Philosophy of Nature,* §250) is outside the Hegelian limits. And this would amount to a great deal. One gets the impression that when Derrida speaks disparagingly of ''closure'' in the Hegelian system, he has in mind the ''syntheses'' of bivalent logic prevalent in nondialectical systems, discussed in chapter 5. But the Hegelian system, if it involves a collapse of the ordinary distinctions between thought and being, also leads to a collapse of the binary distinction between closure and unassimilable otherness (by focusing on that very limited sphere where there is a distinction which is no distinction, or a unity-in-distinction). Thus it envisions more precisely a ''closure of closure and alterity'' analogous to what Hegel calls the ''identity of identity and difference,'' or to the formular completeness of Gödel's Incompleteness Theorem. We are dealing not with synthesis here, but with paradox, in which distinction is not only not dissolved, but perpetuates and intensifies itself.

## *Corollary, Derivative, and Subsidiary Paradoxes*

1. *Corollary paradoxes:* There are certain paradoxical unities-in-distinction (sometimes referred to by Hegel simply as ''unities,'' but with the understanding that they are not simple identifications) which are rather directly and intuitively connected with the Idea of the ''unity'' of thought and being, so that they could be considered corollaries to this central idea. One indication that they are corollaries is the fact that they are referred to rather frequently in various parts of Hegel's work. They appear and reappear continually. The following are some of the chief examples:

A. *Subject and object:*

The Idea may be called, subject-object. . . . [55]

In the system proper the unity of ''subject and object'' or, alternatively, ''subjectivity and objectivity''[56] is used as a roughly synonymous designation of the idea of the unity-in-distinction of being and thought.

In the *Phenomenology,* in the context of constant references to the dialectic between consciousness and self-consciousness, in-itself and for-itself, Hegel often uses ''substance-subject'' terminology, sometimes to refer to the total system of the Idea, which must be presented not only as substance (as in Spinoza's philosophy) but also as subject;[57] but sometimes also in a more specific connotation, e.g., in regard to the notion of a divine substance.[58]

B. *Form and content:*

> The Absolute Idea . . . is the pure form of the concept,
> which intuits its content as its own self.[59]

There is no content without some form, no form which does
not in-form some content. Thus form is inseparable from content, although distinguishable from the content. In the Idea,
thought is *the* form (in the most general sense of ''form'') of
being, while being takes on the aspect of a ''content''. Various
specific stages of the Concept or the Idea may also be referred to
as paradoxical unities of form and content. For example, in the
*Phenomenology,* Force as a manifestation of the emerging
Concept is demonstrated in one place to have its form trans-
muted into content and content into form, thus freeing itself
from the customary differentiation of form and content.[60]

C. *Method and subject-matter:*

> The method which I follow in this system of logic . . .
> is not something distinct from its object and content; for
> it is the inwardness of the content, the dialectic which it
> possesses within itself, which is the mainspring of its
> advance.[61]

> The True . . . is merely the dialectical movement, this
> course that generates itself, going forth from, and re-
> turning to, itself.[62]

Although, as we have seen, Hegel affirms the validity of the
distinction between ''analytic'' and ''synthetic'' method as
applied to the sciences and mathematics, and admires the grand,
if misguided, attempt of Spinoza to produce a synthetic philosophical system, he insists that the analytic-synthetic distinction does not apply at all to a proper system of philosophy. In his
own ''dialectical-speculative'' system, the meanings of ''analytic'' and ''synthetic'' are no longer the same as they are in
finite cognition.[63] The meanings have been fused together. One
could say that his system is ''analytic,'' since it is concerned
with the investigation and differentiation of concepts; but one
could say with equal right that it is ''synthetic,'' since there is a

subject-matter which is organized and assimilated as "other," elaborated and expanded through the Idea.[64] It would be more accurate, however, to drop the terms "analytic" and "synthetic" and to speak of the self-generating method-content of the Idea, which proceeds from its most abstract stages (e.g., the dialectic of Being and Nothingness in Becoming) to its more concrete stages (e.g., the dialectic of consciousness and self-consciousness in Reason).[65] Just as an organism is directed or "programmed" by the inner law of its own self-contained teleology, so also the initial, abstract, quasi-intuitive concept of the interchangeability and mutual transmutability of being and thought *possesses* its *own* self-contained method in a fundamental sense ("method" etymologically derives from the Greek for "way" or "path") which guides its unfolding or progression.

D. *Freedom and necessity:*

> The enrichment [of the content] proceeds in the *necessity* of the Notion. . . . Each new stage of *forthgoing,* that is, of *further determination,* is also a withdrawal inwards. . . . The highest, most concentrated point is the *pure personality* which, solely through the absolute dialectic which is its nature, no less *embraces and holds everything within itself,* because it makes itself the supremely free—the simplicity which is the first immediacy and universality.[66]

In his early comparison of the Fichtean and Schellingean systems, Hegel had insisted that the final philosophy emerging out of these pathfinding efforts would have to be a system synthesizing necessity and freedom, which are not fundamentally opposed to each other but are inseparable correlative aspects of the Absolute Subject-Object.[67] Hegel's later system may be regarded as a lengthy and complex progression from those immediate, abstract stages of the being-thought complexus in which being and the necessity of being are emphasized to the final concrete stages (of the *Philosophy of Spirit*), in which thought and the freedom of thought are emphasized, after having been generated dialectically out of being. In the Concept, necessity and freedom tend to converge. Thus the "necessity" that emerges in conformity with the Concept is not the mechanical necessity accruing to material interactions, but first appears as the "free necessity" of chemical interactions which condition actions and reactions by means of their inner teleology rather than by means of the blind and dead necessity of external manipulation;[68] and the "freedom" congruent to the Concept is not the abstract indetermination of "free choice" or even the more concrete power of self-determination, but the "infinite" freedom which comes to terms with the necessities in its environment and even comes to control them for the establishment and perpetuation of freedom.[69]

2. *Derivative and subsidiary paradoxes:* I have characterized corollary paradoxes as those which are most directly and even intuitively connected with the Idea of the identity-in-difference of being and thought. There are other paradoxes which are also of pivotal importance in Hegel's system but are less self-evidently connected with the Idea. For example, when Hegel portrays the Idea as the "unity . . . of the finite and the infinite, of soul and body; the possibility which has its actuality in its own self; that of which the nature can be thought only as existent,"[70] he is referring to a series of paradoxes which need to be derived by a system of *proof* from the Concept and the Idea, just because they are not intuitively apprehended as variations on, or parallel to, the being-thought correlation. The purpose of the arguments and explanations in Hegel's system is precisely to demonstrate the connection of the Idea with these latter paradoxes, as well as the hundreds of other subsidiary paradoxes which one finds throughout Hegel's philosophical works, some examples of which I have given in chapter 3.[71] I do not wish to maintain that these derivative and subsidiary paradoxes can be sharply and clearly distinguished from the corollary paradoxes, since we are dealing here more with a difference of degree than a difference of kind. I want only to emphasize that it is precisely because these sorts of dialectical "conclusions" are more remotely and indirectly or obliquely connected

with their "premises" that a close textual reading of Hegel's proof-system is necessary, and it is unfortunately not possible, by laying hold on some hitherto inaccessible "secret" of Hegel, to make these more remote nooks and crannies more readily accessible.

## Hegel's System as Paradox: The Circle of Circles

At the end of his Frankfurt period, Hegel believed in the subordination of philosophy, which had to do essentially with the finite, to religion, which alone was able to elevate the finite into the infinite. But at the time of his move to Jena in the early 1800s, he began to see the possibility of a "reflection of reflection," for the attainment of "infinity" within philosophy itself.[72] Under the influential mentorship of Schelling, Hegel began to refer to the possibility of presenting the Absolute as truly "self-grounding."[73] This seminal idea seems to have been still in Hegel's purview as he constructed his later "system" (called an "*Encyclopedia*," with an etymological emphasis on the Greek root, $\varkappa v \varkappa \lambda \acute{o} \varsigma$, "circle"), which could be characterized as an intellectual structure in which the finite reflections of the understanding are reflected into each other dialectically under the aegis of Reason. This highly self-reflective system is described by Hegel as a "circle of circles":

> The whole of philosophy . . . resembles a circle of circles. The Idea appears in each single circle, but, at the same time, the whole Idea is constituted by the system of these peculiar phases, and each is a necessary member of the organization.[74]

This geometrical analogy is found also in the *Science of Logic* and is repeated in the *Philosophy of Nature*.[75] Like most analogies, it could be counterproductive if one were to place too much emphasis on it. However, like many analogies, it can also be a useful instrument for facilitating conceptual comprehension, if properly understood. But in this particular case, the nature of the prime analogate is somewhat problematic. For it is not immediately obvious what is entailed by a "circle of circles," which could mean concentric circles, a spiral, etc. G. H. Haring, for example, interpreted the "circle of circles" motif as circles embedded in a rather stationary manner within larger circles, as in Diagram A.[76]

This diagram gives us an intimation of what Hegel's "circle" analogy probably meant, although it does not accord completely with Hegel's statements to the effect that each circle would "return upon itself,"[77] that each individual circle would "give rise to a wider circle,"[78] and that the "circle of circles" would consist of links"[79] formed from the subordinate circles. Haring also confines himself to Hegel's *Science of Logic* as a circle consisting of the subordinate circles formed by being, essence, and Concept; while Hegel relates the "circle of circles" analogy further and primarily to the system consisting of the three circles formed by the *Logic, Philosophy of Nature,* and *Philosophy of Spirit.*

M. J. Inwood sees the "circle of circle" imagery as an important expression of Hegel's unique conception of philosophy as systematic self-reflection—that is, a massive self-producing, self-justifying, and self-correcting system which demystifies, and works out the concrete details of, Aristotle's primal presentation of the Idea as "self-thinking thought."[80] Hegel's claim about the "circles" of the system returning upon themselves can best be understood, suggests Inwood, as a variation on the concept of "infinite circularity". Some examples given by Inwood: A novel which ends up with its own writing as the climax; assumptions which lead to conclusions justifying the original assumptions, etc.[81] It is in terms of such paradoxical recursions, says Inwood, that we can best understand the thrust of Hegel's *Encyclopedia,* which starts with logic and ends with philosophy, whose beginning lies in logic;

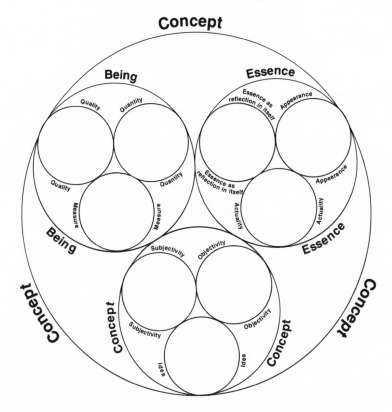

Diagram A

or of Hegel's *Phenomenology,* in which the final stage of consciousness considered is the one capable of examining all its predecessors.

Inwood then shows how the "circle of circle" analogy works itself out into diverse infinite circles in Hegel's *Encyclopedia:* The *Logic, Philosophy of Nature,* and *Philosophy of Spirit* are all circles in the sense that they begin with, and end with, pure being or one of its manifestations, which sets the stage for the next "circle"; the *Logic* is a circle also insofar as it leads to the Absolute Idea, which involves a survey of the whole *Logic,* and this basic pattern—of ending with a survey that takes one back

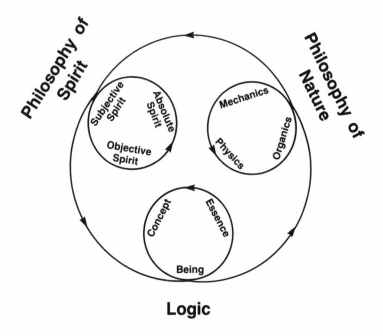

Diagram B

to the beginning—is repeated in the latter two sections of the *Encyclopedia;* the *Philosophy of Spirit* is a circle in a double sense, insofar as its ending involves a return not only to its beginning but to the beginning of the whole *Encyclopedia;* and the system as a totality is a circle insofar as it ends with philosophy, whose culmination is the dialectical-speculative *Logic* with which the *Encyclopedia* begins.[82]

If we were to follow up on the geometrical analogy in line with Inwood's explanation, we might end up with something like Diagram B.

This schema (in which subordinate circles and subcircles are only implicit) does some justice to Hegel's statements, mentioned earlier, and to Inwood's clarification. But it is insufficient, if we wish to take into account Hegel's final restatement of the "circle of circles" analogy in terms of what Pöggeler calls a "system syllogism". [83] In this final account, Hegel goes on to observe that each of the three larger subcircles in the overall circle of the system takes its turn alternatively in serving as a "middle term" for the other two, producing a total structural "syllogism". Thus, if we use L, N, and S to designate the *Logic, Philosophy of Nature,* and *Philosophy of Spirit,* respectively, the first syllogism produced, following Hegel's account, is LNS, in which the Idea of Nature functions as "middle term"; the second is NSL; and the third is SLN. The final picture that Hegel leaves us with is of a tripartite system in which each part is mediating every other part. If we wanted to depict the "circle of circles" model in such a way as to bring out these latter elaborations, we would have to abandon the previous diagram and substitute a configuration in which the "system-circle" is seen as an inner continuity produced by the interaction of the three syllogism-circles, in which the first syllogism holds together L and S through the mediation of N, the second syllogism holds together L and N through S, and so forth, as in Diagram C.

Even if this latter schema is a more accurate depiction of the geometrical analogy, it is, of course, just an analogy. The main defect of Hegel's "circle" analogy is that, like the "paradox of infinity," to which it bears a *prima facie* resemblance, it does not explicitly incorporate the *contradictory* element, or what Hegel called "the power of the negative," which is essential to a *bona fide* paradox, as I argued above, and as Sarlemijn notes in regard to Haring's "circles." [84] And so we must leave the analogy behind to appreciate the fact that Hegel's system as a whole is a true paradox, not only involving a complex network of simultaneous recursions, but simultaneously holding together the overarching, architectonic *oppositions* of being and thought, along with numerous corollary and subsidiary oppositions whose dialectical connections with the originary paradox will be more remotely, and certainly in some cases less convincingly and credibly, necessitated in the unfolding of the overall system-paradox.

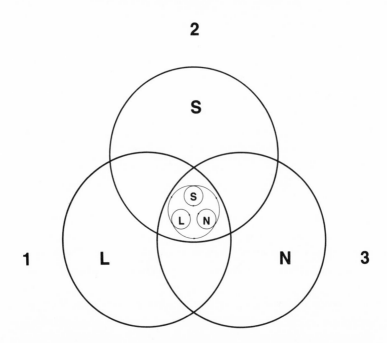

Diagram C

# *Hegel's* Phenomenology of Spirit *and Circularity*

The most thorough treatment of the nature and historical genesis of epistemological circularity in Hegel's system is to be found in Rockmore's *Hegel's Circular Epistemology*.[85] In this book, Rockmore shows how the "anti-foundationalism" of Hegel's final system developed from a problem initially posed by Reinhold, reformulated by Bardili (to whose influence Hegel responded directly), and followed up in a Kantian context by Fichte in great systematic detail.[86] Hegel, following Fichte's lead, developed a circular system which, unlike linear systems, should not need to use shaky "first principles" as the foundation upon which all derivations and arguments would have to be ultimately based. Hegel's strategy was to depend for justification not on antecedent first principles but on (1) an experimental approach to counter the *a priori,* "foundationalist" quest for certitude of Descartes' *cogito;* and (2) an emphasis on practice as a corroboration of theory—a species of corroboration modeled on Descartes' own little-known (and highly inconsistent) approach in part 6 of his *Discourse on Method.*[87] Rockmore concludes, however, that, while Hegel was successful in providing the empirical basis for certainty that Descartes could not provide, he was ultimately unsuccessful in his efforts to make the transition from certainty to truth through his neo-Cartesian pragmatic approach.[88] The basic reason for Hegel's failure, in Rockmore's estimation, was his espousal of an irrationalist, anti-Enlightenment "faith in reason."[89]

To back up this conclusion, Rockmore relies heavily on Hegel's statement in the *Logic* §224 that Reason must start out with an "absolute faith" in its identity with objectivity. This statement in the *Logic* parallels the very similar statement in the *Phenomenology* §§230–33 concerning the immediate certainty of Reason about its union with reality (i.e., about the unity of thought and being). But neither in the *Logic* nor in the *Phenomenology* is this taken to be a matter of mere "faith." In both cases, further argument and development show that the proof for this initial "faith" is to be found in a speculative synthesis of theory and practice. The presentation of the synthesis is the most detailed in the *Phenomenology* M§§394ff., where *die Sache selbst,* Reason's final emergence into an individual consciousness no longer hampered by the discrepancy between the in-itself and the for-itself, or between certitude about the in-itself and the truth of the for-itself, is described, and even defined as "the absolute" (M§420), *not* to be confused with "Absolute Knowledge" (Speculative Philosophy), whose emergence out of the social and cultural consciousness is described several hundred pages later in the *Phenomenology.* This interesting and much misunderstood section on *die Sache selbst,* which portrays a situation (somewhat analogous to the Kierkegaardian "task") in which an individual takes himself and his own ethical milieu as both his practical goal and his prime theoretical interest, would seem to be the final expression that Hegel himself saw as the "truth" corresponding to Reason's initial certitude in M§232. In the *Logic* the parallel synthesis comes with the [theoretical-practical] Absolute Idea (§236). Rockmore, in assessing the success of Hegel's circularity, would have to focus on this self-mediating stage, rather than on a stage of "immediate certainty" in the dialectical development.

Unlike Rockmore, Richard Winfield finds Hegel quite successful in developing an antifoundational approach to truth, even more successful than Rorty, Davidson, and other contemporary would-be antifoundationalists. The dependence of the latter on a coherence theory of truth necessitates some "ultimate context," which functions in a foundational way. Hegel himself, according to Winfield, avoids such an *aporia* by his architectonic idea of knowledge as a result which corroborates its starting point, a representation which is identical with the object represented, and a philosophical standpoint which sums up and explicates the truth of all previous standpoints.[90]

In discussing the "epistemology" of any philosopher, a distinction has to be made, first of all, between (1) his use, possibly implicit, of an epistemology or epistemological presuppositions in his work (e.g., on metaphysics or ethics), and (2) his specific treatment *of* epistemology. Rockmore, in concentrating primarily on Hegel's *Logic* (which is Hegel's response to metaphysics) and on the rest of Hegel's *Encyclopedia,* is considering Hegel's epistemology primarily in the first sense.

Does Hegel have an epistemology in the second sense? Here again a distinction must be made: Just as Hegel's *Logic* is meant to replace metaphysics in the usual sense of the word,[91] so also Hegel's *Phenomenology* is in great part, among other things, Hegel's answer to epistemology. The first half of the *Phenomenology* could well be portrayed as a series of theoretical and practical epistemological dilemmas produced by various natural and historical approaches to certitude and truth, examined by Hegel with methodological skepticism and empirical comprehensiveness for the purpose of establishing an "absolute" standpoint above such dilemmas. These systematic analyses of certitude and truth are not "strictly" an epistemology because they are not concerned with our attainment of truth about the world, or even about "the Absolute," as something distinct from consciousness. Rather, as Hegel makes clear in his Introduction, in order to avoid such scholastic, Cartesian, and Kantian dilemmas, he will be focusing on a special "object" which is never a "thing-in-itself"—namely, self-consciousness itself, which as *self*-consciousness is a *unity* of concept and object and as *consciousness proper* is the *distinction* of concept from object. The *Phenomenology* is concerned with certitude (knowledge) and truth (the objectivity corresponding to knowledge)—traditional topics for treatment in an epistemology— except that the overt "subject-matter" in the *Phenomenology* is restricted to self-consciousness and Spirit, in consideration of which the traditional epistemological stances undergo dialectical and paradoxical reversals. Thus it might be more accurate to characterize the analysis of certitude and truth in the *Phenomenology* as "para-" or as "meta-" epistemological.

It must also be taken into account that, as Pöggeler and Bonsiepen have emphasized, the "dialectic of certitude and truth" seems to be replaced, in the last half of the *Phenomenology* (chapters VI–VIII) with a "dialectic of Substance and Subject." The reason for this is that, as Hegel announced in his Introduction (M§232), the "phenomenology of consciousness" would reach its terminus at that point where there is finally a correspondence between concept and object, certitude and truth. This point is reached in a preliminary way in the chapter on Self-Consciousness (M§174), which possesses an immediate "*certainty* of its *truth*," and in a conclusive way with *die Sache selbst* at that point where the "Absolute Consciousness" is attained (M§420).[92] From that point, which marks the definite transition from the phenomenology of consciousness to the phenomenology of Spirit, the phenomenology is no longer concerned with the quasi-epistemological problem$_1$ of bringing certitude and truth into correspondence, but with the uniquely Hegelian problem$_2$ of showing how this *correspondence* unfolds differentially in the "ethical substance" and in "religion."

The gradually transcended dialectic of certitude and truth, which (as we shall see) provides the basis for the "circularity" of the *Phenomenology*, proceeds in its larger outlines as follows:

A. *Consciousness,* beginning with Sense-Certainty, finds that the truth of Sense-Certainty is in Perception, then that the truth of Perception is in the Understanding (of Force), and finally that the truth of the Understanding (and of Consciousness-in-General) is in the Infinite Concept (*Self*-Consciousness).

B. *Self-Consciousness,* as the truth of Consciousness, begins with the immediate certainty of its truth (M§174), and implements its "Desire" to make *this* certainty explicit and objective through the freedom of self-consciousness from external otherness (attained by transition through the Master-Slave dialectic, stoicism, skepticism, and the Unhappy Consciousness). In finally resolving the dichotomies of the Unhappy Consciousness, it becomes the certitude/truth of Consciousness/Self-Consciousness, i.e., it becomes what Hegel refers to technically as "Reason."

C. *Reason,* then beginning as the certainty of the unity of being and thought, reality and ego, looks for the objective "proof" or truth of *this unity* first (D) through the observation of nature, then (E) in practical self-actualization, and finally (F) in *die Sache selbst,* in which the synthesis of truth and certainty in Reason becomes explicit.

This final synthesis is developed *in the world* first as (G) Spirit, which passes historically from the truth of the synthesis of reason in the Ethical Substance to the certainty of the synthesis in Conscience; and second as (H) Religion, which passes atemporally from the mere certainty of the synthesis of Reason in Nature-Religion to the explicit truth of the synthesis in Revealed Religion. The coordination of both of these transitions (G and H) finally takes place (I) in speculative philosophy (Absolute Knowledge), which gives *conceptual* expression to the perennial *imaginative* representations of Religion. Speculative Philosophy, however, must continually return to its empirical grounding in (A) the phenomenology of Consciousness (see M§806). And so the "epistemological" segments of the circuit begin all over again.

The preceding developments give rise to a *prima facie* "circle of circles," which can be diagrammed in a way analogous to the initial diagram of the "circle of circles" in the *Encyclopedia* (see page 96 above and Diagram D).

However, just as our preliminary *prima facie* interpretation of the *Encyclopedia* had to be supplemented by one which would take into account Hegel's own final self-interpretation in terms of the "syllogism of syllogisms," so also Diagram D on the following page must be supplemented with a view to Hegel's own self-interpretation as expressed primarily in the two massive architectonic recapitulations of the *Phenomenology* at the beginning of the chapters on Religion (M§§679–82) and on Absolute Knowledge (M§§789–93, 798–800). These recapitulations as well as Hegel's other frequent recapitulations and anticipations are essential for a comprehension of the overall structure of the *Phenomenology*.

P.-J. Labarrière has differentiated and categorized these "parallel" structures and movements in his excellent and comprehensive structural and dynamic analysis of the *Phenomenology*.[93] Labarrière's interpretation of the circular developments in the *Phenomenology* explicitly takes into account Hegel's remarks (in the passages just cited above) to the effect that (1) chapters I–VI of the *Phenomenology* constitute the "totality of Spirit" in its "consciousness"; (2) Religion, the "self-consciousness of Spirit," in its own autonomous circular development, gathers together the "universal moments" which in previous sections of the *Phenomenology* were associated with the manifestation of particular "shapes" (*Gestalten*); and (3)

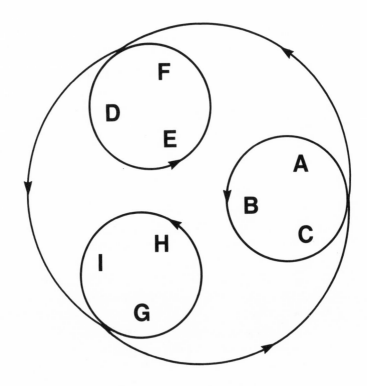

Diagram D

Absolute Knowledge is the unification of (a) the reconciliation of Consciousness with Self-Consciousness in Spirit, and (b) the reconciliation of Self-Consciousness with Consciousness in Religion. If we examine three of Labarrière's illustrative diagrams successively, we will see in the third diagram how Hegel probably understood the final "circularity" of the *Phenomenology*.

Note in Figure 1 that the "totality of Spirit" referred to by Hegel comprises not just chapter VI, *entitled* "Spirit," but chapters I–VI. Note also that the "phenomenology of con-

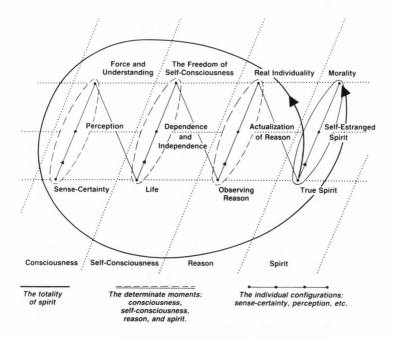

Fig. 1 Spirit's Reconciliation of Consciousness and Self-Consciousness in [Kantian] Morality and [Fichtean] Conscience. (Adapted from Pierre-Jean Labarrière, *Structures et mouvement dialectique dans la* Phénoménologie de l'Esprit *de Hegel* [Paris: Aubier, 1968]. Reprinted with the permission of the author and publisher)

sciousness'' up to and including ''Real Individuality'' provides the background or foundation for Spirit Proper.

In Figure 2 we see how the three stages of Religion are, as Hegel indicates (§681), self-conscious extensions of Spirit in-itself, for-itself, and in-and-for-itself, in a *double* sense: Nature-Religion is a continuation (vertically) of Spirit-in-itself (Consciousness) and *also* (horizontally) of the moments of the ''in-itself'' which pervade Consciousness, Self-Consciousness, and Reason/Spirit; Art-Religion is a continuation not only of Spirit for-itself (Self-Consciousness) but *also* of the abstract

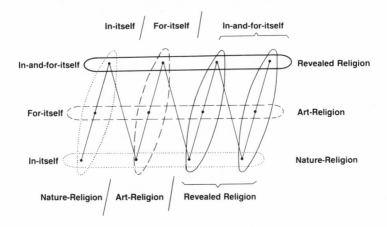

Fig. 2 Religion's Reconciliation of Self-Consciousness and Consciousness in Revealed Religion [Christianity]. (Adapted from Pierre-Jean Labarrière, *Structures et mouvement dialectique dans la* Phénoménologie de l'Esprit *de Hegel* [Paris: Aubier, 1968]. Reprinted with the permission of the author and publisher)

moments of the for-itself in Consciousness, Self-Consciousness, and Reason/Spirit; and Revealed Religion is a continuation not only of Spirit in-and-for-itself (Reason/Spirit) but also the abstract moments of the in-and-for-itself in consciousness, self-consciousness, and reason/spirit, including such figures as the "Suprasensible world" (in consciousness), the "Unhappy Consciousness" (in self-consciousness), and (in Spirit) the "Absolute Being" projected as the reward and rewarder of Kantian morality (see M§§673–76).

Figure 3 depicts how Absolute Knowledge takes for its "Form" the total dialectical circuit of Spirit portrayed in Figure 1, which reaches its highest spiritual form in the Fichtean practical philosophy; and takes its "Content" from the total circuit of Spirit's self-consciousness, i.e., Religion, which acquires its Total Content and final objectification in the Christian community. Absolute Knowledge itself, then, is the final philosophical form given to the main figurative tenets or doctrines of

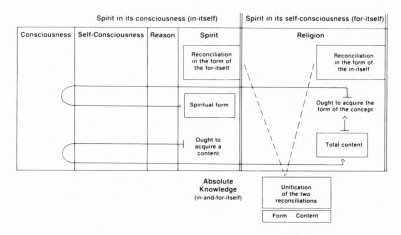

Fig. 3 Absolute Knowledge as the Reflection of Reflection, or the Reconciliation of the Two Reconciles. (Adapted from Pierre-Jean Labarrière, *Structures et mouvement dialectique dans la* Phénoménologie de l'Esprit *de Hegel* [Paris: Aubier, 1968]. Reprinted with permission of the author and publisher)

the Christian religion, which functions as the speculative content.[94]

One obstacle to an understanding of the highly organized circular structure of the *Phenomenology* has been a lack of attention to the basic triadic networking which is the generator of the "circularity" in this work. The tremendous surge of books on the *Phenomenology* in the last ten years[95] may be partly due to the fact that the *Phenomenology,* with less of the incessant explicit triads than the *Encyclopedia,* is more attractive to professional interpreters in an intellectual milieu where formalism and rationalism are looked down upon. But triads and subtriads there are, not only the ones that Hegel explicitly announces in the titles and subtitles, but implicit triads from the very beginning, e.g., in the first chapter, "Sense-Certainty," (1) the essentiality of the object (M§93), (2) the essentiality of the ego (M§101), and (3) the essentiality of reciprocity between ego and object (M§103); and in the third type of reciprocity a subtriad (M§107) of (a) the "now," (b) the negation of the "now" (the "has been"), and (c) the "negation of the negation" (the reinstatement of a universal "now"). Literally hundreds of examples could be given, but one still finds commentators claiming, possibly out of embarrassment, that Hegel put no stock in "triplicity."[96]

Another impediment to the understanding of the overall circular structure of the *Phenomenology* is the unwarranted claim, first proposed by Theodore Haering, that the last sections of the *Phenomenology* were largely long, hastily written, and erratic afterthoughts, not in line with Hegel's original intentions. The most recent proponent of this thesis is Robert Solomon, who quotes "Pöggeler" (no source given) as in agreement with Haering and himself.[97] This reference to Otto Pöggeler is strange, since Pöggeler, while allowing that there was a shift of emphasis during the writing of the *Phenomenology*,[98] resolutely rejects Haering's thesis.[99] One who accepts Haering's thesis would, of course, be averse to recognizing any circularity in the *Phenomenology* as a whole.

There is evidence that Hegel believed his eight years as a high-school instructor and principal helped him to achieve greater clarity as a philosopher. An increase in clarity is noticeable in the *Encyclopedia,* insofar as editorial cues—subtitles, etc.—are supplied to the grateful reader to help break up the complex arguments into their natural divisions. But the earlier *Phenomenology,* lacking such cues, and also bulging in some places from a wealth of material, while overly lean in other places, nevertheless is a sustained dialectical development of thought like the *Encyclopedia,* and results, like the latter, in a circular system or, perhaps more precisely, a circular reflection of the system.[100]

## Circularity and Philosophical Paradox

At the end of W. T. Stace's well-known *Hegel,* which is a paraphrase of Hegel's *Encyclopedia,* there is a massive fold-out chart which delineates all the triads, subtriads, sub-subtriads, etc., of Hegel's mature System. Used as a ready-reference guide to contents, such a chart might be useful, but it is also a threat to the proper understanding of Hegel, insofar as it presents the *Encyclopedia* as a linear, and indeed formalistic, system.

We help to minimize this theoretical threat by presenting the *Encyclopedia* and/or the *Phenomenology,* in accord with Hegel's own metaphorical characterization, as a "circle," or even a "circle of circles," and also, as was mentioned above,[101] by recognizing the contradictory or paradoxical element in this circularity. But here again, it is necessary to emphasize the difference between logical-semantical and philosophical paradox, discussed in chapter 3. If, for example, Hegel's systematic circularity is understood after the manner of the standard logical paradoxes of "infinite circularity" (as a cursory reading of some of Inwood's examples might imply[102]), Hegel's system cannot escape from the shadow of suspicion of being a *"circulus vitiosus."* Such a circle of course would constitute no improvement over the defects germane to linear systematicity. And so at this point it is necessary to reemphasize the fact that systematic circularity in Hegel is of a special sort—the dialectical circularity of philosophical paradox, in which two opposed or contradictory ideas are joined together in such a way that they complement and confirm each other, and transform themselves into each other. Philosophical paradox is the inseparable concomitant to circularity in both the *Phenomenology* and the *Encyclopedia.*

To sum up: In the *Phenomenology,* the primary, overarching paradox is the transformation in our experience (and in Spirit in general) of consciousness into self-consciousness, substance into subject, and vice versa. In the *Encyclopedia,* the pivotal paradox is the unity-in-distinction of the thought of being (in the Logic) and the being of thought (beginning in the Philosophy of Nature and finding fullest expression in the cultural and historical analyses of the Philosophy of Spirit). And it is noteworthy that in the latter opus, what started out as an oxymoron with Parmenides—that it is the same thing to be, and to be thought—

is transformed into the most massive and sustained instance in
the history of philosophy of the systematic dialectical development of a conceptual paradox.

# Conclusion

In this book I have focused my attention on paradox, dialectic, and system as three factors, each of which is important in its own right and bears some significant relationships to the others, especially in Hegel's system. If we were to confine our attention to the fourth and fifth forms of dialectic considered in chapter 4—in which opposition in and among ideas is entailed—it would seem that almost any combination of the three factors is possible, and/or actually achieved. For example, we could say that with Nicholas of Cusa we have paradox and the rudiments of systematization, with a minimum of explicitly dialectical argumentation; Kant's "Transcendental Dialectic" is a manifestation of dialectic without paradox in the strict sense (as holding together opposites) and without incorporation into a system; the "dialectical materialism" of Engels and the "historical materialism" of Marx give us an eclectic use of dialectic in a not-completely dialectical system of socioeconomic criticism, generating intermittent ironies, contradictions, and reversals, but without the bourgeois solace of metaphysical paradoxes which incorporate the oppositions which they transcend; in Kierkegaard we certainly find some remnants of a reinterpreted Hegelian dialectic and dialectical terminology (e.g., between the different elements of the self, between the concrete and the abstract, the "in-itself" and the "for-itself") and some metaphysical paradoxes, as well as the peculiarly Kierkegaardian revision of paradox (Christianity as *the* paradox), but a resolute opposition to the idea of a philosophical system; in Nietzsche we find multifarious paradoxes, not only in the aphorisms but in the books and essays, but without any explicit attention to dialectical methodology, and, like Kierkegaard, an aversion to systems; and in the works of the British neo-Hegelian F. H. Bradley we encounter an elaborate, somewhat monistic system which—more like Plato than Hegel—attempts to transcend the contradictions of the world to attain a nonparadoxical, nondialectical vision of idealized reality. Finally, in the work of some contemporary poststructuralists and hermeneuticists, we encounter interesting philological analyses of the generation of dialectic and paradoxes, and (in Derrida's work) a paradoxical concept of an infrastructural system of differences impervious to, and subversive of, dialectical systematization. (The latter position is particularly difficult to maintain, since it could easily be mistaken for an anti-system, and thus living proof of the sort of dialectical opposition it wants to get away from.)

In contrast to all these efforts in modern philosophy, Hegel combined all three elements—paradox, dialectic, and system—to create a unique and rather ingenious homeostasis. And this, indeed, seems to be his peculiar contribution (but also, as Hegel himself grants, a contribution indebted to the efforts of his predecessor Fichte and his early collaborator Schelling) to modern philosophy. As a by-product of this main contribution, Hegel also gives us an interesting model of what a complete *and* consistent philosophical system—if such a thing be possible—might look like.

Earlier in this book, we saw that it is highly doubtful whether Hegel's dialectic could be formalized. This is because "formalization" conceptually is germane to a more traditional logic, in which a strong distinction between "form" and "content" is assumed. But, *servatis servandis,* the triadic development that we find in Hegel's system is itself perhaps the closest approximation to "formalization" one could hope to find in a dialectical system. In keeping, however, with Hegel's refusal to separate form and content, *this* "formalization" is intentionally entwined with its content, instead of being presented as a system of inference rules, variables, constants, and operators. Thus, if one were to try to produce the sort of system for which Hegel is noted, some nonformalistic employment of what Hegel called "the method of triplicity" might be required—although not necessarily to the extent that it is employed by Hegel.

In our time there is an immense interest in dialectic and "dialectics." Every month or so another book having to do in some way with this subject sees the light of day. But—as also is the case with words like "democracy" and "philosophy" itself—one finds that a wide variety of often incompatible meanings are parading around in the dress of univocity. The thrust of this book has been to the effect that dialectic, in its higher stages of development, is inseparably intertwined with paradox. For example, a dialectical "synthesis" which merged opposites (as in a compromise) instead of retaining and perpetuating a clash of opposites (as in a paradox) would be suspect. An additional implication of the position defended in this book is that the frequently lamented failure of philosophy up through the centuries to come up with a single universally (or even generally) accepted truth may be due to the traditional avoidance, by "mainstream" philosophers, of philosophical paradox and the dialectic that is associated with it. In other words, it may be the case that our sole moderately satisfactory hope of presenting the more important philosophical truths is through paradoxes. The fact that Hegel, by a kind of instinct of reason, inched into the formulation of a system in which the "Absolute Idea" would, when properly attended to, systematize *itself* instead of requiring our arbitrarily devised systematizations, brings us to the absolute limits of "system-building" itself, but not to the interdiction of further attempts at the systematization of dialectic.

# Notes

## Chapter 1

1. J. N. Findlay, "Goedelian Sentences: A Non-Numerical Approach," in *Mind* 51 (1942).

2. V. W. Quine, "New Foundations for Mathematical Logic," *American Mathematical Monthly* (February 1937).

3. Eric Toms, *Being, Negation and Logic* (Oxford: Basil Blackwell, 1962), 7.

4. Toms, 11–13, 15–16.

5. In *Mind* (1963).

6. Toms, 52–54.

7. Graham Priest, "The Logic of Paradox," *The Journal of Philosophical Logic* 8 (1979): 219–41. According to Priest, we should follow Hegel to "dialetheia"—allowing some statements to be both true and false. See S. Bartlett and P. Suber, eds., *Self-Reference* (Dordrecht: Nijhoff, 1987).

8. Toms, 81ff.

9. Ibid., 6.

10. Stéphane Lupasco, *Logique et contradiction* (Paris, 1947), and *L'energie et la matière physique* (Paris, 1974).

11. G. Melhuish, *The Paradoxical Nature of Reality* (Bristol: St. Vincent's Press, 1973).

12. See page 4.

13. J. R. Lucas, "Minds, Machines, and Gödel," *Philosophy* 36 (1961): 112.

14. Melhuish, 53–54.

15. Ibid., 57.

16. Ibid., 3–8, 18–19, 25.

17. G. W. F. Hegel, *Logic,* trans. William Wallace (Oxford: University Press, 1965), 213. Errol Harris, supporting Hegel's interpretation of the law

of identity, observes: "If *A* is *A*, the second *A* is not the first (and if it were no proposition would be enunciable); so it should really be written, *A* is *A'*. . . . And if *A* is *A'*, '*A* is not non-*A* (=*A'*)' is false." See *An Interpretation of Hegel's Logic* (New York and London: University Press of America, 1983), 166–67.

18. Ibid., 221. Observes Harris (ibid.): "To say that *A* is not *X* is to say that it is something else. Its A-ness depends on and is constituted by what it excludes and is not, but only if that is something positive and complementary to it in a larger whole. If not to be non-*A* is a bare negative, if it has no positive significance, then it is not *A*. On the other hand, what are complementary in a larger whole are not mutually exclusive so far as they are mutually constitutive, and the either-or of the understanding does not apply to them."

19. *Logic,* 220, 69.

20. Ludwig Wittgenstein, *Tractatus Logico-Philosophicus,* 5.5303.

21. Toms, 55.

22. Nicholas Rescher and Robert Brandom, *The Logic of Inconsistency* (Oxford, 1980).

23. Toms, 43.

24. Melhuish, 102.

25. Leslie Armour, *Logic and Reality: An Investigation into the Idea of a Dialectical System* (Assen: Van Gorcum, 1972), 3, 10–12. Toms, Armour et al. have been primarily concerned with using an immanent critique of ordinary logic to bring out its unavoidable limitations. A more fundamental approach is essayed by Burkhard Tuschling of Marburg University, West Germany, in "Widerspruch und Konsistenz," forthcoming in *Zeitschrift für philosophische Forschung,* 1988. In the advance copy which I received, Tuschling, building on the logical theory of Jan Lukasiewicz, shows that the classical bivalent propositional calculus with its emphasis on analyticity requires an abstraction from "a more complex reality, in which 'analytic' and 'synthetic' concepts are inseparably interwoven." He concludes that the "law of contradiction" and other presuppositions in logic are relativized by the possibility of complementing bivalent logic with a non-bivalent logic.

26. Cf. Thomas Kuhn, *The Structure of Scientific Revolutions* (Chicago, 1962), 138–39, 150–51, 158–59.

## Chapter 2

1. Eric Toms, *Being, Negation and Logic,* 54–55.

2. See the *Phenomenology,* trans. Miller, Introduction, #84ff. Wolfgang Janke (*Historische Dialektik: Destruktion dialektischer Grundformen von Kant bix Marx* [Berlin and New York: de Gruyter, 1977], 30ff.) also, following Hegel, locates the source or core of dialectic in self-consciousness, but understands by "self-consciousness" the rather advanced stage of Hegel's

*Phenomenology* in which self-consciousness has become a "we" which divides up into the unequal, antagonistic extremes of Master and Slave. It is a matter of some debate whether this stage involves the arbitrary introduction of external, historical material into the dialectic. But in any case, it must be kept in mind that the *whole* of the *Phenomenology* is an analysis by consciousness of its own conscious knowledge, i.e., an analysis of self-consciousness by itself, an analysis which is intrinsically associated with the generation of dialectic, as Hegel demonstrates in detail in M§§86–87 of the Introduction.

3. If "I" is ordinary logic based on the principle of identity, and "∼I" is a dialectical logic based on a principle of nonidentity, then a congruent metatheorem of dialectical logic would be [I ↔ ∼I].

4. See Michael Kosok, "The Formalization of Hegel's Dialectical Logic," *International Philosophical Quarterly* 6, 4 (1966), 531; Yvon Gauthier, "Logique hégélienne et formalisation," *Dialogue* 6, 2 (1967); Stéphane Lupasco, *Logique et contradiction* (Paris, 1947); Dominique Dubarle and André Doz, *Logique et dialectique* (Paris, 1972); and Jaakko Hintikka, "The Logic of Information-Seeking Dialogues: A Model," *Konzepte des Dialektik,* Eds. W. Becker and W. Essler (Frankfurt am Main: Vittorio Klostermann, 1981), 212–30.

5. George Melhuish, *The Paradoxical Nature of Reality,* xiv.

6. Toms, 120ff. See also Melhuish, 44–45.

7. Melhuish, 42.

8. Ibid., 81, 86–97.

9. Leslie Armour, *Logic and Reality,* 17.

10. See, e.g., his *Logic,* 143ff.

# Chapter 3

1. The comparison could be carried a bit further here: Some paradoxes are completely argued and worked out, e.g., the paradox that being is identical with nothingness elaborated at the beginning of Hegel's *Logic,* and these would be comparable to a completed syllogism in ordinary logic; other paradoxes give hints as to their justification, without giving the complete argument, and these would be comparable to enthymemes in logic.

2. See Rosalie Colie, *Paradoxia Epidemica: The Renaissance Tradition of Paradox* (Princeton, N.J.: Princeton University Press, 1966).

3. Kierkegaard, *Journals and Papers,* trans. Hong, vol. 3 (University of Indiana Press, 1975), #3072, #3073.

4. Colie, 9.

5. Hegel, *Lectures on the History of Philosophy,* III, 531.

6. Colie, 9.

7. Ibid., chap. 15. According to Colie, following Lando, the stock Renaissance paradoxes were: Poverty is better than riches; it is better to be

ignorant than learned; it is better to be blind than to have sight; it is better to be
mad than wise; it is not a bad thing for a prince to lose his state; it is better to
live in exile than to languish in one's native land; it is better to weep than to
laugh; it is better to live in a cottage than in a great palace; it is neither shameful
nor odious to be a bastard; it is better to be in prison than at liberty; a frugal life
is better than a splendid and sumptuous one; and it is better to have no servants
than to have them.

8. We are allowing ourselves the luxury of considering pure forms here.
But there are, of course, hybrids. Some of Chesterton's paradoxes (e.g., "The
Christians of the Middle Ages were only at peace about everything—they
were at war about everything else") are literary from the point of view of their
style and context, but philosophical insofar as they are actually argued for at
length. The paradoxes appearing in philosophical-fictional work such as
More's *Utopia*, Kierkegaard's "Diary of a Seducer" in *Either/Or*, I, or
Nietzsche's *Thus Spake Zarathustra* would be of the same genre.

9. See Hegel's *Phenomenology*, the chapter on "The Observation of
Nature," ad. fin.

10. Ibid., the chapter on "Absolute Freedom."

11. See the *Philosophy of Right*, #280, Addition.

12. See the *Logic*, 119.

13. Hegel, *Phenomenology*, trans. Miller, §§188, 343, 753.

14. *Either/Or*, I, "The Unhappiest Man" and "The Rotation Method."

15. See pages 15–17 above.

## Chapter 4

1. Hegel, *Science of Logic*, II, 3–2, A(b) 2 (801).

2. Hegel, *Natural Law*, trans. Knox (University of Pennsylvania Press,
1975), 62.

3. Kant, *Critique of Pure Reason*, A151 = B191.

4. Ibid., A156 = B195.

5. See Ludwig von Bertalanffy, *General Systems Theory* (New York:
Braziller, 1968); and, by the same author, "An Outline of General Systems
Theory," *British Journal for the Philosophy of Science* I (1950): 134–65.
There is not complete agreement about the origins of GST. Jonathan Turner,
for example, argues that the sociological application of GST began in the
nineteenth century with Herbert Spencer's *First Principles*. See Jonathan H.
Turner, *Herbert Spencer: A Renewed Appreciation* (Beverly Hills, Calif.,
London, and New Dehli: Sage Publications, 1985), chap. 3.

6. Erwin Laszlo, *Introduction to Systems Philosophy: Toward a New
Paradigm of Contemporary Thought* (London and New York: Gordon and
Breach, Science Publishers, 1972), 3.

7. Erwin Laszlo, *Systems Science and World Order: Selected Studies*

(Oxford and New York: Pergamon Press, 1983), 39.

8. *Introduction to Systems Philosophy*, 12.

9. See page 31 above.

10. See *Phänomenologie des Geistes*, 34.

11. See pages 32 and 36 above.

12. See page 31 above.

13. See page 32 above.

14. *Lectures on the History of Philosophy*, I, 396.

15. Richard Rorty, *Philosophy and the Mirror of Nature* (Oxford and Princeton, N.J.: Basil Blackwell and Princeton University Press, 1979), 264.

16. See ibid., 367ff.

17. See Jacques Derrida, "Différance," in his *Margins of Philosophy*, trans. A. Bass (Chicago: University of Chicago Press, 1982), 1–28. See also "Tympan," ibid., xxiii, and David Hoy, *The Return of Grand Theory in the Human Sciences*, ed. Quentin Skinner (Cambridge: Cambridge University Press, 1985), 43ff.

18. Jacques Derrida, *Of Grammatology*, trans. G. Spivak (Baltimore: Johns Hopkins University Press, 1976), 46.

19. Jacques Derrida, *Speech and Phenomena*, trans. D. B. Allison (Evanston: Northwestern University Press, 1973), 149.

20. Rodolphe Gasché, *The Tain of the Mirror: Derrida and the Philosophy of Reflection* (Cambridge and London: Harvard University Press, 1986), 180.

21. Michael McCanles, "The Dialectical Structure of Discourse," *Poetics Today* 3, 4 (1982): 21–37.

22. See Gregory Vlastos, "The Socratic Elenchus," in *Oxford Studies in Ancient Philosophy*, ed. J. Annas (Oxford: Clarendon Press, 1983), 52 ff.; and "Afterthoughts . . . ," ibid., 74.

23. See Plato, *Republic* 511b, 533c, 534b, 534e.

24. See H. Kainz, "The Use of Dialectic and Dialogue in Ethics—A Reflection on Methodology," in *The New Scholasticism LVI*, 2 (Spring 1982).

25. Jaakko Hintikka, "The Logic of Information-Seeking Dialogues: A Model," in *Konzepte des Dialektik*, eds. W. Becker and W. Essler (Frankfurt am Main: Vittorio Klostermann, 1981), 212–30. Dialectic for Hintikka is a method rather than a logic, and the particularly appropriate model for it is the question-and-answer dialogue. Dialectic thus becomes the art of asking questions in such a way as to ensure engagement and progress between the agents involved. The process can also be applied by extension to self-questioning— e.g., the questions concerning *anamnesis* posed by Plato, the questions concerning preexisting knowledge posed by Aristotle, and the self-questioning of the Absolute evolving to self-awareness in Hegel's metaphysics (see ibid., 228).

26. See G. E. L. Owen, *Logic, Science and Dialectic: Collected Papers in Greek Philosophy* (Ithaca: Cornell University Press, 1986), 222–23, 238. See

also Niels Jørgen Green-Pedersen, *The Tradition of the Topics in the Middle Ages: The Commentaries on Aristotle's and Boethius' "Topics"* (Munich: Philosophia Verlag, 1984), 15–19.

27. See Adler's explanation of his "dialectical" approach in *The Idea of Freedom: A Dialectical Extension of the Conception of Freedom* (Garden City, N.Y.: Doubleday, 1958), chap. 5.

28. See Marshall McLuhan, *Understanding Media* (New York: Signet, 1964), 88ff.

29. Prior to Luther, Cicero utilized a similar approach in a limited manner in his *Paradoxa stoicorum*. Following Luther, Sebastian Franck is noted for the most profuse systematization of paradox, as a vehicle primarily for interpretation of Scripture (see Franck's *280 Paradoxes or Wondrous Sayings*, trans. E. J. Furch [Lewiston, N.Y.: Edwin Mellen Press, 1986]). I have adopted and adapted this methodology of Luther (and Franck) in chapter 2 of *Wittenberg Revisited: A Polymorphous Critique of Religion and Theology* (Washington, D.C.: University Press of America, 1981).

30. See Jasper Hopkins, *Nicholas of Cusa's Metaphysic of Contraction* (Minneapolis: The Arthur J. Banning Press, 1983).

31. See H. Rehder, "Of Structure and Symbol: The Significance of Hegel's *Phenomenology* for Literary Criticism," in *A Hegel Symposium*, ed. J. Travis (Austin: University of Texas Press, 1962), 133.

32. See *Lectures on the History of Philosophy*, I, 278ff.

33. See the *Logic*, §81, Remark.

34. See Kant's *Critique of Pure Reason* (A426 = B454, ff.).

35. See the *Logic*, §81, Remark.

36. Karl Marx and Friedrich Engels, *Selected Correspondence*, trans. Dona Torr (New York: International Publishers, 1942), 246.

37. See György Andrassy, "Marx's Philosophy of History and Hegel's Logic," *Studia Philosophica et Sociologia Auctoritate Universitatis Pécs Publicata* (Pécs, Hungary, 1983); Richard Winfield, "The Logic of Marx's *Capital*," *Telos* 27 (Spring 1976); and Jindrich Zelený, *The Logic of Marx*, trans. T. Carver (Totowa, N.J.: Rowman and Littlefield, 1980).

38. See, e.g., Engels's *Socialism: Utopian and Scientific*, section II. Marx in a letter to Laura and Paul Lafargue, 15 February 1869, distinguishes Darwin's theory from "Darwinism." In particular, Marx rejected Darwin's Malthusianism and emphasized the questionable anthropomorphism of the "struggle for existence". But Marx also explicitly gives evidence of Darwinian methodological suppositions, e.g., in *Capital*, trans. Fowkes (N.Y.: Random House, 1977), 92, 459, 493n, and in his insistence that what a Russian reviewer had described as a "natural-science" approach was his own non-Hegelian, realistic form of "dialectics," ibid., 100–102. For a discussion of a common "functionalist" explanatory methodology in Darwin and Marx, see G. A. Cohen, *Karl Marx's Theory of History* (Princeton, N.J.: Princeton University Press, 1978), 271, 285–91. On Marx's "natural-sci-

ence'' approach to social theory, and the controversies concerning this interpretation of Marx, see Bruce Mazlish, *The Meaning of Karl Marx* (Oxford: The University Press, 1984), 17, 132, 160n, 168n; Peter Worsley, *Marx and Marxism* (London and New York: Tavistock-Methuen, 1982), chapter 3; Paul Heyer, *Nature, Human Nature, and Society: Marx, Darwin, Biology, and the Human Sciences* (Westport, Conn.: Greenwood Press, 1982), 47–49, 54–57, 65–68; Lewis S. Feuer, ''The Case of the 'Darwin-Marx' Letter: A Study in Socio-Literary Detection,'' *Encounter*, October 1978, 76–78; and Mark Warren, ''On Ball, 'Marx and Darwin: A Reconsideration,' '' *Political Theory* 9, 5 (May 1981): 260–63.

39. Thomas Sowell, *Marxism: Philosophy and Economics* (New York: William Morrow–Quill, 1985), 14–15.

40. Richard Norman and Sean Sayers, *Hegel, Marx and Dialectic: A Debate* (New Jersey and Sussex: Humanities Press and Harvester Press, 1980), 106–8.

41. Norman Levine, *Dialogue Within the Dialectic* (London: Allen and Unwin, 1984), 125n.

42. Op. cit., Introduction.

43. Scott Meikle, ''Dialectical Contradiction and Necessity,'' in J. Mepham and David-Hillel Ruben, eds., *Dialectics and Method* (Brighton, Sussex: Harvester Press, 1979), 19–20.

44. Norman and Sayers, *Hegel, Marx and Dialectic*, 167.

45. Georg Lukács, *History and Class Consciousness* (Cambridge, Mass.: MIT Press, 1971), 24; Alfred Schmidt, *The Concept of Nature in Marx*, trans. Fowkes (London: NLB, 1971), 61; David-Hillel Ruben, ''Marxism and Dialectics,'' in Mepham and Ruben, eds., *Dialectics and Method*.

46. Eduardo Vásquez, Qué es la Dialéctica (Caracas, Venezuela: Editorial de la Universidad Simón Bolívar, 1986), 41–42.

47. Lucio Colletti, *Marxism and Hegel* (London and New York: NLB and Schocken Books, 1973), chap. I; Alfred Schmidt, *The Concept of Nature in Marx*, 166–67.

48. Daniel Little, *The Scientific Marx* (Minneapolis: University of Minnesota Press, 1986), 112–22.

49. Richard Hudelson, ''Marxist Science as Ordinary Science,'' *Nous* 20, 1 (March 1986).

50. Jacques Guillaumaud, ''Sauver la dialectique?'' *Science et dialectique chez Hegel et Marx*, ed. M. Vadée (Paris: Editions du Centre National de la Recherche scientifique, 1980), 85, 89–90, 93.

51. Klaus Hartmann, *Die marxische Theorie* (Berlin: de Gruyter, 1970), 21–25.

52. See Guillaumaud, ''Sauver la dialectique?'' 86.

53. *Logic*, §48, Remark.

54. *Philosophy of Nature*, §119, Remark #2.

55. *Science of Logic*, 150.

56. Ibid., 151.

57. William Maker, "Hegel's Critique of Marx: The Fetishism of Dialectics," paper presented at the Hegel Society of America conference, Atlanta, October 1986; forthcoming in *Hegel and His Critics*, Donald Verene, ed. (Albany: State University of New York Press, 1988). See also Hegel, *Logic* §43; *Philosophy of Nature*, §§213, 247.

58. Ibid., p. 25 of the HSA conference draft.

59. See *Phenomenology*, M§§29–30; *Logic*, §213; *Science of Logic*, 725.

60. See the *Science of Logic*, 47; see also Immanuel Fichte, *Grundzüge zum System der Philosophie* (Heidelberg, 1933), I, 308.

61. See Joseph O'Malley, "Marx's 'Economics' and Hegel's *Philosophy of Right:* An Essay on Marx's Hegelianism," *Political Studies* 24, 1 (March 1976): 43–56.

62. An interesting parallel to Marx's eclecticism in regard to dialectic is to be found in his similarly eclectic theory of morality or justice. In response to ongoing disputes about Marx's theory of justice (or lack of such a theory), Steven Lukes, in *Marxism and Morality* (Oxford: Clarendon, 1985), chap. 4, offers a solution in terms of Marx's eclectic combination of (1) insights about capitalist norms of justice; (2) immanent ethical critique of these norms; (3) external critique in terms of emerging socialist norms; and (4) radical critique in terms of an ultimate communist society which would transcend "justice" *and* "injustice"—concepts germane only to a class-based society. Hence the difficulty of saying what Marx means by "justice."

63. Richard Levins and Richard Lewontin, *The Dialectical Biologist* (Cambridge: Harvard University Press, 1985). Similar endeavors at dialectical-empirical systematizations are to be found in Stéphane Lupasco, *Les trois Matières* (Strasbourg: Editions Coherence, 1982), a work largely independent of Marxist moorings; and in Errol E. Harris, *Formal, Transcendental and Dialectical Thinking* (Albany: State University of New York Press, 1987), Part III, an interweaving of Hegelianism with contemporary science.

## Chapter 5

1. See Otto Pöggeler, "G. W. F. Hegel: Philosophie als System," in *Grundprobleme der grossen Philosophen*, ed. J. Speck (Göttingen: Vandenhoeck and Ruprecht, 1972), 155.

2. See *Faith and Knowledge*, trans. Cerf and Harris (Albany, N.Y.: SUNY, 1977), 168ff.

3. Hegel, *The Science of Logic*, Preface to the First Edition.

4. See H. Kainz, *Hegel's Phenomenology, Part I* (Tuscaloosa: University of Alabama Press, 1976), 11–14.

5. Hegel, *The Berlin Phenomenology*, trans. and ed. M. J. Petry (Boston and Dordrecht: Reidel, 1981), Introduction, xvii–xviii.

6. Denise Souche-Dagues, *Le circle hégélien* (Paris: Presses Universitaires de France, 1986), 17.

7. See section C, Method and subject-matter, pages 90–91 above.

8. See the *Logic*, §§226ff.

9. See Immanuel Kant, *Critique of Pure Reason*, A150 = B190ff.

10. See ibid., B115, B395, B416–19.

11. See the *Logic*, §§226ff.

12. Hegel, *The Science of Logic*, II, 3–2, A(b) 2, 801.

13. Hegel, "Ausführung des teleologischen Beweises in den Vorlesungen über Religionphilosophie vom Sommer 1831," in *Werke* (Suhrkamp Verlag), XVII, 520.

14. Hegel, *Logic*, §§229, 231.

15. Hegel, *The Philosophy of Right*, §211, Addition.

16. Hegel, *Logic*, §231 (italics added).

17. See ibid., §229, Remark, §231, and *The Science of Logic*, 536–37, 581–82, 815.

18. See *Logic*, §227.

19. *Lectures on the History of Philosophy*, I, 38.

20. Ibid., II, 229.

21. Ibid., 38.

22. *The Difference Between Fichte's and Schelling's System of Philosophy*, Preface, 82.

23. *Lectures on the History of Philosophy*, III, 486.

24. *The Phenomenology of Spirit*, §238.

25. *Lectures on the History of Philosophy*, III, 521.

26. Ibid., 525.

27. Ibid., 526.

28. Ibid., 542.

29. *The Phenomenology of Spirit*, §9, §804.

30. *Logic*, §13.

31. See Aristotle, *Metaphysics XII*, 9, 1074b.

32. *Lectures on the History of Philosophy*, II, 229.

33. *The Philosophy of Mind*, §573.

34. *Lectures on the History of Philosophy*, III, 479.

35. *Logic*, §14.

36. *Lectures on the History of Philosophy*, I, 39, and III, 552; *Logic*, §13. This concept of one system developing in history is of course the rationale behind Hegel's reference to the "system" of Fichte and Schelling in the title of the *Differenzschrift*, rather than to the "systems."

37. See pages 26ff. above.

38. See *Difference Between Fichte's and Schelling's System of Philosophy*, 81.

39. Ibid., 82.

40. See ibid., 157–64, 187; *Lectures on the History of Philosophy*, 551.

41. See *The Science of Logic*, 758; *Logic*, §214.

42. See *The Science of Logic*, 755, 758.

43. Ibid., 600.

44. Ibid., 755.

45. *Logic*, 14–15.

46. *Lectures on the History of Philosophy*, III, 409.

47. See *The Science of Logic*, 48, and Otto Pöggeler, "G. W. F. Hegel: Philosophie als System," *Grundprobleme der grossen Philosophen*, 160.

48. For a discussion of this ambiguity, see my *Hegel's Phenomenology, Part I*, 11–14.

49. *The Phenomenology of Spirit*, §85.

50. This completes only a rough sketch of thought-being themes in the *Phenomenology*. For a somewhat more detailed outline of the whole *Phenomenology*, see my *Hegel's Phenomenology, Part II* (Athens, Ohio: Ohio University Press, 1983), 2–8.

51. See the *Logic*, *The Science of Logic*, and *The Philosophy of Nature*, trans. A. V. Miller (Oxford, 1970); and *The Philosophy of Mind*, trans. Wallace and Millar (Oxford, 1971).

52. See George D. O'Brien, *Hegel on Reason and History: A Contemporary Interpretation* (Chicago and London: University of Chicago Press, 1975), 65–67. See also Alfred Schmidt, *The Concept of Nature in Marx*, 189.

53. Being would be a first-order phenomenon; the thought of Being second-order; and the unity-in-distinction of the two third-order.

54. Jacques Derrida, *The Margins of Philosophy*, trans. Alan Bass (Chicago: University of Chicago Press, 1982), ixff., 19–20, 94; and *Writing and Difference*, trans. Alan Bass (Chicago: University of Chicago Press, 1978), 273–77.

55. See the *Logic*, §214.

56. See, e.g., the *Logic*, §82, Remark.

57. See, e.g., *The Phenomenology of Spirit*, M§17.

58. See ibid., M§748.

59. *Logic*, §237.

60. See the *Phenomenology*, M§140ff.

61. *Science of Logic*, 54.

62. The *Phenomenology*, M§65.

63. *Science of Logic*, 830–31.

64. Ibid., 838.

65. Ibid., 801; *Logic*, §88; *The Philosophy of Mind*, §§436–39. E. Coreth sees the fusion of analysis and synthesis as the essence of Hegel's dialectical methodology. See Coreth's *Das dialektische Sein in Hegel's Logik* (Vienna, 1952), 20, 25.

66. *Science of Logic*, 841.

67. See *The Difference Between Fichte's and Schelling's System of Philosophy*, 167ff.

68. *Science of Logic*, 725–26.
69. *The Philosophy of Right*, §§22–29.
70. *Logic*, §214.
71. See pages 36 and 38–39 above.
72. See Otto Pöggeler, "G. W. F. Hegel . . . ," 155.
73. Hegel, *The Difference Between Fichte's and Schelling's System of Philosophy*, 113.
74. *Logic*, §15; see also §17.
75. See *The Science of Logic*, 842; *The Philosophy of Nature*, Introduction and §342, Remarks.
76. See the chart at the end of C. L. Michelet and G. H. Haring, *Historisch-kritische Darstellung der dialektischen Methode Hegels*, reprint (Hildesheim: Gerstenberg Verlag, 1977). Haring's innermost subcircles are omitted from this reproduction.
77. *Science of Logic*, 842.
78. *Logic*, §15.
79. *Science of Logic*, 842.
80. See M. J. Inwood, *Hegel* (London and Boston: Routledge and Kegan Paul, 1983), 271–76, 547–48.
81. Ibid., 149–55.
82. Ibid., 317ff.
83. *Philosophy of Mind*, §574ff; Pöggeler, "G. W. F. Hegel . . . ," 177. Mitchell Aboulafia's exposition of paragraphs 574ff. in *The Self-Winding Circle: A Study of Hegel's System* (St. Louis, Mo.: Warren Green, 1982), 19ff., is flawed by his attempt to make sense out of the Wallace translation, which reads *trennt sich* instead of *trennt sie* in §575, so that nature is said to "sunder *itself*," instead of "separate *them* (the two extremes)"—as would be more natural to the middle term of a "syllogism."
84. See pages 7–8 above, and Andries Sarlemijn, *Hegel's Dialectic* (Dordrecht and Boston: Reidel, 1975), 8.
85. Tom Rockmore, *Hegel's Circular Epistemology* (Bloomington: Indiana University Press, 1986).
86. Ibid., 27–41.
87. Ibid.
88. Ibid., 158.
89. Ibid., 156.
90. Richard Dien Winfield, "Hegel versus the New Orthodoxy," paper presented at the Hegel Society of America conference, Atlanta, October 1986.
91. *Logic*, §28, Remark.
92. Otto Pöggeler, *Hegels Idee einer Phänomenologie des Geistes* (Freiburg: Alber, 1973), 222, and Wolfgang Bonsiepen's "Editorischer Bericht" in the Akademie edition of the *Phänomenologie*, 467. Hegel himself in a fragment from 1805 says "Das absolute Wissen tritt so zuerst als gesetzgebende Vernunft auf" (Bonsiepen, 437).

93. Pierre-Jean Labarrière, *Structures et mouvement dialectique dans la Phénoménologie de l'Esprit de Hegel* (Paris: Aubier, 1968). See the appendixes of Labarrière's book for the parallels.

94. For further detail on the genesis and implications of these final overall developments, see Labarrière, *Structures et mouvement*, 145–214, and Kainz, *Hegel's Phenomenology, Part II*, 125–31, 172–86. On the overall progressive development of the in-itself and for-itself throughout the *Phenomenology*, see Kainz, *Hegel's Phenomenology, Part I*, 164–65.

95. See Thomas Lutzow and H. Kainz, "Recent Work in Hegel," *American Philosophical Quarterly* 16, 4 (October 1979): 273–85; and H. Kainz, "Recent Interpretations of Hegel's *Phenomenology*," *Hegel Studien* 16 (1981): 245–51. Many more books on the *Phenomenology* have come out since these review articles were published.

96. Donald Verene's insightful but impressionistic *Hegel's Recollection* (Albany: State University of New York, 1985), citing Hegel's critique of the formalistic use of "triplicity" in M§50, equates triplicity with the "thesis-antithesis-synthesis legend." However, Hegel in M§50 and elsewhere only criticizes the misuse of "triplicity," which had been characterized as the "Absolute Method" by Schelling (see Bonsiepen and Heede's *Anmerkungen* in the Akademie edition, Band 9, of the *Phänomenologie*, 490). Hegel goes on to characterize this "Absolute Method" as a means by which, when properly used, "the true form with its true content have been presented together, and the Concept of Science has become explicit" (M§50; see also the *Logic*, §230, Remark). The omnipresence of the formula "in-itself, for-itself, in-and-for-itself" is Hegel's substitute for the "thesis-antithesis-synthesis" terminology. Some of the implicit triads are brought out by Hyppolite's editorial divisions in his French translation of the *Phenomenology* and by Baillie in his Table of Contents for the English translation, although one cannot always rely on their interpretations. It seems best to acknowledge that Hegel did indeed have a streak of formalism and pedantry; but no more so than Aquinas in his *Summa theologiae*, Spinoza in his *Ethics*, or Wittgenstein in his *Tractatus Logico-Philosophicus*.

97. Robert Solomon, *In the Spirit of Hegel* (Oxford and New York: Oxford University Press, 1983), 212–14, 156.

98. See Pöggeler, "Zur Deutung der Phänomenologie des Geistes," *Hegels Idee einer Phänomenologie*, 221.

99. Pöggeler, in the same article to which Solomon (p. 214n) refers, characterizes Haering's thesis as "absurd" (*Hegels Idee . . .* 194) and "inconsistent" (207n.), and accuses Haering of distorting Hegel's meaning and using faulty philological methods (192–205). Comments Pöggeler: "Ich stelle fest: es gibt keinen Beweis dafür, dass die *Phän.* ursprünglich nur bis zum Kapitel Vernunft hat reichen sollen. Haring ist zu seiner Hypothese nur gekommen, weil es von vorherein auf die spätere, verkürzte Fassung der *Phän.* gesehen hat" (205).

100. See M§805. Pöggeler observes (ibid., 222, 226) that when Hegel wrote this reference to a *Phenomenology*-System "correspondence" he was no doubt thinking of his projected system as sketched in his *Realphilosophie* of 1805/6. See also Bonsiepen, "Editorischer Bericht," 467. But Robert Grant McRae, *Philosophy and the Absolute* (The Hague: Nijhoff, 1985), 31f., 41, has pointed out that there is also at least a rough correspondence between the parts of the *Phenomenology* and the parts of the later *Encyclopedia*. If so, Souche-Dagues's reference to the *Phenomenology* as the "system reflected in consciousness" (see page 78 above) seems an appropriate way to characterize the disputed relationship between the *Phenomenology* and the System proper.

101. See above, page 97.

102. See above, page 94.

# Bibliography

Adler, Mortimer. *The Idea of Freedom: A Dialectical Extension of the Conception of Freedom*. Garden City, N.Y.: Doubleday, 1958.

Armour, Leslie. *Logic and Reality: An Investigation into the Idea of a Dialectical System*. Assen: Van Gorcum, 1972.

Bartlett, Steven J., and Peter Suber, eds., *Self-Reference*. Dordrecht: Nijhoff, 1987.

Bertalanffy, Ludwig von. *General Systems Theory*. New York: Braziller, 1968.

———. "An Outline of General Systems Theory." *British Journal for the Philosophy of Science* I (1950).

Colie, Rosalie. *Paradoxia Epidemica: The Renaissance Tradition of Paradox*. Princeton, N.J.: Princeton University Press, 1966.

Coreth, E. *Das dialektische Sein in Hegel's Logik*. Vienna, 1952.

Dubarle, Dominique, and André Doz. *Logique et dialectique*. Paris, 1972.

Findlay, J. N. "Goedelian Sentences: A Non-Numerical Approach." *Mind* 51 (1942).

Gauthier, Yvon. "Logique hégélienne et formalisation." *Dialogue* 6, 2 (1967).

Guillaumaud, J. "Sauver la dialectique?" *Science et dialectique chez Hegel et Marx*, ed. M. Vadées. Paris: Editions du Centre National de la Recherche scientifique, 1980.

Hartmann, Klaus. *Die Marxische Theorie*. Berlin: de Gruyter, 1970.

Hegel. *The Difference Between Fichte's and Schelling's System of Philosophy*, trans. Harris and Cerf. Albany, N.Y.: SUNY, 1977.

———. *Lectures on the History of Philosophy*, 3 vols., trans. Haldane. London: Routledge and Kegan Paul, 1968.

———. *Logic,* trans. William Wallace. Oxford: University Press, 1965.

———. *Natural Law,* trans. Knox. Philadelphia: University of Pennsylvania Press, 1976.

———. *The Phenomenology of Spirit,* trans. Miller. Oxford: Oxford University Press, 1977.

———. The *Philosophy of Right,* trans. Knox. Oxford: University Press, 1952.

———. *The Science of Logic,* trans. Miller. New York: Humanities Press, 1969.

———. *Werke.* Frankfurt am Main: Surkamp Verlag, 1969.

Hopkins, Jasper. *Nicholas of Cusa's Metaphysic of Contraction.* Minneapolis: The Arthur J. Banning Press, 1983.

Inwood, M. J. *Hegel.* London and Boston: Routledge and Kegan Paul, 1983.

Kainz, Howard. *Hegel's Phenomenology, Part I.* Tuscaloosa: University of Alabama Press, 1976; second printing, 1979; reprinted 1988 by Ohio University Press, Athens, Ohio.

———. *Hegel's Phenomenology, Part II.* Athens, Ohio: Ohio University Press, 1983.

———. ''The Use of Dialectic and Dialogue in Ethics—A Reflection on Methodology.'' *The New Scholasticism LVI,* 2 (1982).

Kant, Immanuel. *Critique of Pure Reason,* trans. Norman Kemp Smith. New York: St. Martin's Press, 1965.

Kierkegaard, Søren. *Either/Or,* 2 vols., trans. Swenson. New York: Anchor-Doubleday, 1959.

———. *Journals and Papers,* vol. 3, trans. Hong. Bloomington: Indiana University Press, 1975.

Kosok, Michael. ''The Formalization of Hegel's Dialectical Logic.'' *International Philosophical Quarterly* 6, 4 (1966).

Kuhn, Thomas. *The Structure of Scientific Revolutions.* Chicago: University of Chicago Press, 1962.

Labarrière, Pierre-Jean. *Structures et Mouvement dialectique dans la* Phénoménologie de l'Esprit *de Hegel.* Paris: Aubier, 1968.

Laszlo, Erwin. *Introduction to Systems Philosophy: Toward a New Paradigm of Contemporary Thought.* London and New York: Gordon and Breach, Science Publishers, 1972.

———. *Systems Science and World Order: Selected Studies.* Oxford and New York: Pergamon Press, 1983.

Little, Daniel. *The Scientific Marx*. Minneapolis: University of Minnesota Press, 1986.

Lucas, J. R. "Minds, Machines and Gödel." *Philosophy* 36 (1961).

Lupasco, Stéphane. *Logique et Contradiction*. Paris, 1947.

―――. *L'energie et la matière physique*. Paris, 1974.

McLuhan, Marshall. *Understanding Media*. New York: Signet, 1964.

McRae, Robert Grant. *Philosophy and the Absolute*. The Hague: Nijhoff, 1985.

Mazlish, Bruce. *The Meaning of Karl Marx*. Oxford: The University Press, 1984.

Melhuish, George. *The Paradoxical Nature of Reality*. Bristol: St. Vincent's Press, 1973.

Pöggeler, Otto. "G. W. F. Hegel: Philosophie als System." In *Grundprobleme der grossen Philosophen,* ed. J. Speck. Göttingen: Vandenhoeck and Ruprecht, 1982.

―――. *Hegels Idee einer Phänomenologie des Geistes*. Freiburg: Alber, 1973.

Priest, Graham. "The Logic of Paradox." *The Journal of Philosophical Logic* 8 (1979): 219–41.

Rehder, H. "Of Structure and Symbol: The Significance of Hegel's *Phenomenology* for Literary Criticism." In *A Hegel Symposium,* ed. J. Travis. Austin: University of Texas Press, 1962.

Rescher, Nicholas, and Robert Brandom. *The Logic of Inconsistency*. Oxford: Oxford University Press, 1980.

Rockmore, Tom. *Hegel's Circular Epistemology*. Bloomington: Indiana University Press, 1986.

Rorty, Richard. *Philosophy and the Mirror of Nature*. Oxford and Princeton, N.J.: Basil Blackwell and Princeton University Press, 1980.

Sarlemijn, Andries. *Hegel's Dialectic*. Dordrecht and Boston: Reidel, 1975.

Schmidt, Alfred. *The Concept of Nature in Marx*. London: NLB, 1971.

Souche-Dagues, Denise. *Le cercle hégélien*. Paris: Presses Universitaires de France, 1986.

Toms, Eric. *Being, Negation and Logic*. Oxford: Basil Blackwell, 1962.

Vlastos, Gregory. "The Socratic Elenchus." In *Oxford Studies in Ancient Philosophy,* J. Annas, ed. Oxford: Clarendon Press, 1983.

White, Alan. "Achilles at the Shooting Gallery." *Mind* 72 (1963).

Wittgenstein, Ludwig. *Tractatus Logico-Philosophicus,* trans. Pears and McGuinness. London: Routledge and Kegan Paul, 1961.

# Index of Names

Adler, Mortimer, 63
Althusser, Louis, 69
Anaximander, 63
Aquinas, Thomas, 63, 125
Aristotle, 7, 8, 13, 14, 16, 17, 26, 28,
    31, 55, 56, 62–64, 81, 82, 94
Armour, Leslie, 19, 32, 57

Bardili, Christoph, 98
Bergson, Henri, 55, 56
Black, Max, 5, 7
Blake, William, 41
Bohr, Niels, 11, 12
Bonsiepen, Wolfgang, 101, 124, 125
Born, Max, 13
Bradley, F. H., 7, 26
Bruno, Giordano, 38, 64, 77

Capra, Fritjof, 51
Chesterton, G. K., 117
Church, Alonzo, 10
Cicero, Marcus Tullius, 119
Colletti, Lucio, 69
Congreve, William, 40
Cusanus (Nicholas of Cusa), 38, 43, 64,
    65, 77, 111

Darwin, Charles, 68, 87, 119
Davidson, Donald, 100
Derrida, Jacques, 58–60, 62, 88, 112
Descartes, René, 14, 28–29, 39, 46,
    58, 81, 99, 101
Dewey, John, 58
Donne, John, 41

Eckhart, Meister, 40
Einstein, Albert, 12
Eliot, T. S., 41
Engels, Friedrich, 67–72, 111
Epimenides, 2
Eubulides, 2

Fichte, Johann Gottlieb, 55, 65, 66, 77,
    81, 82, 84, 86, 91, 98, 112
Findlay, John, 4, 6
Flaubert, Gustave, 62
Foucault, Michel, 60
Franck, Sebastian, 119
Frege, Gottlob, 58
Freud, Sigmund, 25, 59

Gadamer, Hans-Georg, 59, 60, 62
Galbraith, John Kenneth, 51
Gasché, Rodolphe, 59
Gauthier, Yvon, 31
Genet, Jean, 62
Gödel, Kurt, 4, 6, 10, 11, 14, 20, 31,
    50, 54, 74, 89
Grelling, Kurt, 8
Guillaumaud, Jacques, 69

Haering, Theodore, 108, 125
Haring, G. H., 94, 97
Harris, Errol, 121
Hartmann, Klaus, 70
Hegel: 29; and the Aristotelian syllo-
    gism, 16; and the identity of identity
    and difference, 27, 36, 39; and the in-
    terrelationship of paradox, dialectic,

and system, 111–12; Aristotelian and Platonic dialectic in, 65; "closure" in, 58, 88; the complementarity of the two logics in, 31, 33; defects of system in, 32; dialectical-paradoxical system of, 75–110; influence of Kantian "antinomies" on, 66; on analysis and synthesis, 53, 58; on completeness, consistency, 50–51, 55, 74, 77, 81, 83; on Socratic dialogue, 57; religious persuasion of, 70; unconsciousness of paradox, 38
Heidegger, Martin, 58, 62
Heisenberg, Werner, 11, 12, 14, 46
Heraclitus, 31–32, 38, 56, 57, 63, 65
Hintikka, Jaakko, 62
Hoffstadter, Douglas, 51
Homer, 61
Hopkins, Jasper, 65
Hudelson, Richard, 69
Hume, David, 39
Husserl, Edmund, 58
Hyppolite, Jean, 125

Inwood, M.J., 94

Jacobi, F. H., 65
James, William, 58
Janke, Wolfgang, 115
Jourdain, P. E. B., 6
Jung, Carl, 43

Kant, Immanuel, 23, 39, 44, 52, 58, 62, 66, 77, 82, 84, 86, 98, 101, 106, 111
Kierkegaard, Søren, 38, 44, 58, 100, 111
Kosak, Michael, 31
Kuhn, Thomas, 20, 87

Labarrière, Pierre-Jean, 103–7, 125
Laszlo, Erwin, 54
Lenin, Vladimir, 68
Levine, Norman, 68, 69
Levins, Richard, 73
Lewontin, Richard, 73
Little, Daniel, 69
Locke, John, 80

Lowell, Thomas, 68
Lucas, J. R., 10, 11
Lukács, Georg, 69
Lupasco, Stéphane, 9, 14, 31
Luther, Martin, 64

McCanles, Michael, 60
McLuhan, Marshall, 64
McRae, Robert Grant, 126
Maker, William, 71
Marx, Karl, 66–74, 111, 119
Meikle, Scott, 69
Melanchthon, Philipp, 64
Melhuish, George, 9, 14, 31–32, 56–57
Mill, J. S., 43, 44
More, Thomas, 117

Nicholas of Cusa. See Cusanus
Nietzsche, Friedrich, 57, 112
Norman, Richard, 69

Owen, G. E. L., 118

Parmenides, 46, 61, 63, 109
Petry, Michael, 77
Plato, 7, 17, 29, 38, 39, 55, 56, 60–62, 63, 81, 112
Pöggeler, Otto, 101, 108, 125, 126
Popper, Karl, 6
Priest, Graham, 8
Protagoras, 61

Quine, V. W., 3, 5, 20

Reinhold, Karl, 98
Rescher, Nicholas, 16, 17
Rockmore, Tom, 98–100
Rorty, Richard, 58, 60, 100
Rousseau, Jean-Jacques, 62
Ruben, David-Hillel, 69
Russell, Bertrand, 5, 6, 7, 26, 58
Ryle, Gilbert, 2, 5

Sarlemijn, Andries, 97
Sartre, Jean-Paul, 28–29, 43, 62
Sayers, Jean, 68
Schelling, F. J. W., 33, 39, 65, 66, 77, 80, 81, 82, 84, 91, 112, 125

Schmidt, Alfred, 69
Schrödinger, Erwin, 13
Sève, Lucien, 60
Shakespeare, William, 41
Socrates, 38, 57–60, 61, 63
Solomon, Robert, 70, 108, 125
Souche-Dagues, Denise, 78, 126
Spencer, Herbert, 117
Spinoza, Benedict, 55, 80, 83, 89, 90, 125
Stace, W. T., 108
Stalin, Josef, 68, 69

Tarski, Alfred, 10
Teilhard de Chardin, Pierre, 45, 51
Thales, 63
Toms, Eric, 5, 7, 9, 16, 19, 26, 31–32
Toynbee, Arnold, 51
Turing, A. M., 10

Tuschling, Burkhard, 115

Unamuno, Miguel de, 43
Ushenko, A., 5, 7

Vásquez, Eduardo, 69
Verene, Donald, 125
Vlastos, Gregory, 60
Von Bertalanffy, Ludwig, 53
Von Neumann, John, 5

White, Alan, 7
Whitehead, Alfred North, 55
Winfield, Richard, 100
Wittgenstein, Ludwig, 15, 16, 45, 58, 125
Wolff, Christian, 80

Zeno, 7, 14, 57

# Index of Subjects

*A posteriori,* the, 78
*A priori,* the, 23, 50, 78, 99
"Absolute," the, 99, 101
Absolute knowledge, 33, 65, 83, 86, 99–100, 103, 104, 106
Actuality, 38
Analysis and synthesis, 18, 47–48, 51–54, 64, 80; in Hegel, 31, 32, 36, 56, 67, 75–78, 83, 89, 90–91; in Kant, 52, 78; in Socrates, 57
Analytic and synthetic methods, 76, 80, 90
Analytical truths, 15
Animism, 23
Antifoundationalism. *See* Foundations
Aphorisms, 58, 112
Aristotelian dialectic, 62–64, 65, 66
Art, 43
*Aufhebung,* 32

Being and consciousness, 28–29
Being and nothingness, 14, 28–29, 43, 44, 86, 91
Being and thought: as a third-order phenomenon, 88; as a unity, 37, 46, 80, 84–85, 88–89, 99, 102; in Kant, 86; progressions in the *Encyclopedia,* 86–87, 95, 97; themes in the *Phenomenology,* 85–87
Bell's Theorem, 12

Capitalism, 73
Causality, 12, 27f.

Change, 14. *See also* Movement
Circularity: and paradox, 108–10; epistemological, 98; in Hegel's *Encyclopedia,* 93–98, 109; in the *Phenomenology,* 98–108, 109; nonvicious, 21, 43; vicious, 6, 43
Communism, 73
Complementarity Principle, 12
Completeness. *See* Consistency vs. completeness
Concept, Hegelian meaning of, 84, 85
Conscience, 86, 102
Consciousness, 45; vs. self-consciousness, 22, 101, 102, 104, 105–6, 109
Consistency: in logic, 16, 31; vs. completeness, 10, 20–21, 50–52, 55, 74, 77, 81, 83, 112
Contradiction: in discourse, 60; in Hegel, 70; in logical paradox, 7, 8, 25, 26, 45, 97; in Marxism, 67, 73; law of (non-), 14ff., 25, 31
Creation *ex nihilo,* 18

Deconstruction, 58–60
Demonstrability of paradoxes, 40, 44
Demonstrative pronouns and adjectives, 3, 6
Dialectic. *See* Logic, dialectical
Dialectical: inversions, 73; materialism, 68, 69, 73, 111; progression, 72
Dialectics, 68–69, 74
Dialogue, 57–60, 62, 64, 66, 118
Difference and similarity, 45

Eclecticism in Marx, 72, 73, 121
Ecology, 53
Enlightenment, the, 23, 67, 99
Enthymemes, 116
Epistemology, 59, 98–102
Essence and existence, 43, 44
Everet-Wheeler hypothesis, 16
Evolution, theory of, 68, 69, 72, 87
Excluded Middle, law of, 14ff., 24
Existentialism, 28

Fact vs. value, 26, 54
Feynman diagrams, 12
Field theory, 12, 53
Form and content, 33, 37, 39, 81, 83, 90, 112
Formalism, 50–51, 55, 80, 109, 125
Formalization, 31, 33, 112
Foundations and antifoundationalism, 48, 76, 93, 98–100
Freedom, 36; and necessity, 91; and nothingness, 28

General systems theory, 53, 54
Generalists, 51–54, 88
God, 29, 38, 40
Grammar and usage, 2–10, 20, 37

Hegelian dialectic, 65, 66
Hegelianism, 36, 112
Hermeneutics, 59, 60, 112
Historical materialism, 68, 111

Idea, Hegelian meaning of, 84–87, 91, 94–95, 100, 113
Idealism, 23, 36, 67, 71, 81, 112
Identity, 46, 65; and difference, 27; logical law of, 14ff.; second-order, 27
Immanence and transcendence, 29, 43–44
Immortality. *See* Mortality
Incompleteness Theorem, 4, 10, 11, 14, 20, 31, 89
Intuition: in dialectical logic, 46; in logic, 18; Schelling and, 81
Intuitionism, 33
Irony, 42, 111

Language: and logic, 45; dubious use in paradox-solutions, 5; first-order, 14; second-order, 13
Laws: dialectical, 69, 73; of logic, *see* Logic; of science, 20
Logic: and laws of induction, 19; and rules of inference, 7, 18, 23, 24, 34, 48; conservatism in, 20; dialectical (paradoxical), 9, 14, 16, 19–21, 22–26, 48, 64; hypothetical propositions in, 7; laws of, 14–20, 23, 36; limits of, 74; negation in, 18; ordinary (non-dialectical), 9, 10, 14, 17, 19–21, 22–26, 48, 64; relationship between ordinary and dialectical, 30–33, 45, 57; syllogistic, 16, 28; theorems of, 45, 48

Malthusianism, 119
Maoism, 73
Marxism, 67–74
Materialism, 11, 25
Meaning, 5
Metaphilosophy, 55
Metaphysics, 18, 59, 65, 100, 111
Metascience, 55
Method and subject-matter, 33, 71, 90–91
Middle terms, reflexivity of, 16
Mind and brain, 11, 43, 54
*Modus ponens,* 18
Mortality and immortality, 17, 24, 29, 40, 43
Movement, 28, 36, 38
Mysticism, 31

Necessity, 1, 9, 17, 31
Negation: absolute, 24; negation of, 72, 80; self-consciousness and, 29
Negative facts, 18
New Critics, 38
Newtonian physics, 11, 12, 14
Noncontradiction. *See* Contradiction
Nothingness, 24, 28–29
Number theory, 4, 20

Objectivity. *See* Subjectivity and objectivity

Organisms, 45, 73, 87
Oxymorons, 40, 109

Paradigm(s): in dialectical logic, 46, 58; in science, 20
Paradox(es): "Achilles," 7, 14; and argument, 40; and irony, 42; "barber," 3, 43; bisected, 6; Bradley's, 7, 26; epistemological, 47; examples of, in Hegel's philosophy, 42–44, 75–76; first-order, 4; Hegel's system as, 93–108; in dialectical logic, 35–48; "Lewis Carroll," 7, 16; "liar," 2, 4, 6, 10, 43; literary, 10, 37, 40–42; logical and semantic, 1–10, 25, 37, 42, 43, 109; negative-reflexive, 18; of infinity, 7, 26, 97, 109; of judgment, 16; of negation, 18; philosophical, 10, 35–48, 109; religious, 10, 29, 37, 40, 42; Russell's, 6, 26; second-order, 4, 26; systematization of, 64–65, 66; "third man," 7; vs. "synthesis," 88–89, 113
Parody, 58
Phenomenology, 25
*Phenomenology of Spirit,* place in Hegel's system, 77, 85, 126
Philosophy: as "conversation," 58, 60; as "edification," 58
Platonic dialectic, 60–62, 65, 66
Possibility. *See* Reality and possibility
Potency, Aristotelian, 13, 14, 18–19
Predicate calculus, 10, 79
Probability, 13
Propositions: first-order, 19; monadic assertorial, iii, 36; second-order, 19
Psychology: analytic, 47; developmental, 23

Quantum physics, 11–14, 16, 20

Rational, the: contrasted with empirical, 55, 70; contrasted with faith, 77
Rationalism, 39, 81
Realism, 70
Reality: and possibility, 12, 65; applicability of logic to, 21; as a Hegelian category, 71; conceptions of

objective, 11, 23, 29, 58, 70, 84; first-order, 13; second-order, 13; *see also* Actuality
Reason, Hegelian meaning of, 84, 85, 87, 91, 102, 105–6
Reciprocity, 28, 44
Reflection, 16, 26–30, 36, 77, 93, 94
Religion, 86, 93, 102, 104, 105, 106; Christian, 29, 38, 86, 103, 107, 111; oriental, 29, 40
Religious paradoxes. *See* Paradox(es)
Renaissance, 23, 41, 64
Romanticism, 33

Satire, 58
Scholasticism, 55, 63, 101
Science: empirical, 50, 55, 68, 69, 70; philosophical, 76
Self-consciousness, 22–34, 44, 83–84, 86, 94, 103, 116; vs. consciousness. *See* Consciousness
Self-reference, 6, 7, 8, 16, 20, 21, 25, 26
Self-thinking thought in Aristotle, 26, 82, 94
Sets, 4, 6
Similarity and difference, 44
Skepticism, 23, 77
Socratic: dialogue, 57–60, 61, 66; *elenchus,* 57
Solipsism, 23
Soul, 11, 17, 65
Specialization, 51–54, 88
"Speculative" philosophy, 33, 42, 90, 99, 103, 107
Spirit, 71, 86, 101, 102, 103, 104, 105
Stoicism, 23
Structuralism, 60, 112
Subjectivism, 77, 81, 84, 86
Subjectivity and Objectivity, 11, 23
Subject-Object, the, 84, 91
Substance and Subject, 89, 101, 109
Synthesis. *See* Analysis and synthesis
Synthetic method. *See* Analytic and synthetic methods
System(s): artificial intelligence, 10; Hegel's paradoxical, 75–110; limita-

tions of, 10; limits of the construction of, 113; nonphilosophical, 78–80; of ciphers, 59; philosophical, 49, 54–56, 112; "reflective," 77; single perennial, 83, 85; strong, 10; -syllogism, 97; systematicity of, 59; three constructions of, in Hegel, 78

Tautology, 18, 45, 48
Thing-in-itself, 44, 77, 84, 86, 101
Thomism, 63
Time, 12, 32
Tokens, 5
Transcendence. *See* Immanence and transcendence

Triplicity, 107–8, 109, 112–13, 125
Truth: and certitude, 101–2; coherence theory of, 100; eschewed by Rorty and Derrida, 60; in Hegel's system, 90; propositional conceptions of, 5; Schelling's objective conception of, 81; transcendental, 61
Type theory, 5, 7

Uncertainty Principle, 12, 13, 14, 46
Unity, 45

Value. *See* Fact vs. value

World-order theory, 53